Jacket copy and forwards copyright © 2023 by Tom Kelchner

ISBN: 978-1-7345955-2-9

1. COOKING / Regional & Ethnic / American / Southern States
2. COOKING / Specific Ingredients / Seafood

Tom Kelchner also is the author of:

To Great Grandmother's House We Go; American Comfort Food from the 1970s, 60s and before

Chicamacomico Cookery, Facsimile Edition

Chicamacomico Cookery, Volume 2
Facsimile Edition

Tom Kelchner

Forward to Chicamacomico Cookery, Volume Two, Facsimile Edition

Chicamacomico Cookery Volume Two is uniquely valuable, if for no other reason, for its chapter of wonderful Outer Banks seafood recipes. Filling 16 pages, it's the largest chapter in the 81-page charity cookbook. *Volume Two* was probably published between 1980 and 1983 by the Chicamacomico Banks Volunteer Fire Department Ladies Auxiliary in the communities of Rodanthe and Waves on the North Carolina Outer Banks.

Cookery is valuable for another reason. Since there was a Volume One, published between 1971 and 1974, a comparison with Volume Two speaks volumes (if that isn't too bad a joke) about the decade of changes in the foodways and local culture of the tiny community that produced the two books. We can estimate that Volume Two was published between 1980 and 1983 because it contains an advertisement on the last page for Sun Realty, (established in 1980) and lists a contributor, Lucretia Midgett, who died at age 87 in July of 1983.[1]

Rodanthe had been relatively remote for much of its history. The stretch of barrier island from Nags Head south to Hatteras had only been served by ferry service across the Oregon Inlet until the Herbert C. Bonner bridge was finished in November, 1963.[2]

That means that the massive development and other changes that have swept the Outer Banks were just beginning. I know. I drove NC 12 down that remote and beautiful strip of land in 1964. I returned again 30 years later when my wife and I started vacationing on the Outer Banks in the 1990s.

1. "Other Deaths," *News and Observer*, Raleigh, North Carolina, Mar. 22, 1974, pp 31
2. Carr, Dawson, *NC 12; Gateway to the Outer Banks* (Chapel Hill; University of North Carolina Press, 2016) pp 63

For fewer than 10 years after the bridge opened, the people who lived on the barrier island south of the inlet clearly retained the cooking heritage of their forebearers. Recipes like Chicamacomico Boiled Old Drum stew (which calls for salt pork), Baked Sea Squab, braised Wild Duck and Wild Goose Stew were common enough, that members of the ladies' auxiliary included them in *Volume One* of their fund-raising cookbook. Five recipes in the book begin with the words "old fashioned."

Volume Two, from the 1980s, shows a vision that was looking out to the larger world. In *Volume One* there were no Asian or Italian-style recipes. *Volume Two* includes: Japanese Chicken, Italian Spaghetti Sauce, Quiche Lorraine, Clams Casino, Louisiana Crab Gumbo, Hawaiian Cake, Mississippi Mud Cake, Italian Delight, Angie's Mexican Rice, Zabaglione, the nationally famous Green Bean Casserole (1955) and the iconic Watergate Salad (circa 1975).

Changes in the world of women also are on display in *Volume Two* reflecting the intense decade of campaigning for women's equality. In *Volume One*, 33 percent (21) of the 63 contributors listed their names as "Mrs. (husband's name)." In *Volume Two*, only five percent (four women) out of 84 contributors listed their name as their husband's names plus "Mrs."

There must have been a major change in the organization as well. Only seven of the contributors to Volume One are listed with recipes in *Volume Two*.

The two volumes are full of recipes that obviously were important to families in a tiny community, on a historic barrier island, in one of the most storm-swept places in the United States. They are unique and deserve to be preserved. We hope that these facsimile editions will help keep alive the memories of the people and the history of Chicamacomico, North Carolina.

Forward to the Chicamacomico Cookery Facsimile Edition, Volume One

This is much more than a reprint of a 1960s volunteer fire company charity cookbook. This is the record of an effort to support a life-saving organization in a North Carolina Outer Banks community with a heritage of spectacular heroism.

Today the Chicamacomico Banks Volunteer Fire Department in Rodanthe, North Carolina, is still providing heroic rescues routinely, largely for tourists who get swept into deep water by rip tides or fall victim to medical emergencies. There also are (very rare) shark attacks. Rip tides, heart attacks and shark attacks are sometimes fatal, so, there is nothing routine about the volunteers' "routine."

In the backs of the minds of the volunteers must be the image of the spectacular 1918 rescue of the British crew from a burning tanker, HMS Mirlo, that had been torpedoed by a German submarine seven miles off shore. Captain John Allen Midgett, head of the Chicamacomico Life Saving Station, and his crew struggled through rough seas to rescue the men -- six from an overturned lifeboat in a sea of flaming fuel. They then helped the 42 survivors of the action to safety.

In 1921, the British government awarded Gold Lifesaving Medals for "Gallantry and Humanity in Saving Life at Sea" to the rescuers. The incident is accepted as the most spectacular rescue in Life-Saving Service/Coast Guard history.

The North Carolina Outer Banks is a wonderful and unique place. The people who have lived on those barrier islands for more than 300 years sometimes struggled to find enough to eat, but they have always used their ingenuity to turn the wonderful fish, game and other foods available to them into great meals.

Sometime between 1963 and 1974, the Ladies Auxiliary of the Chicamacomico Banks Volunteer Fire Department of Rodanthe rounded up 197 recipes, many unique to their families and the Outer Banks, and published a fund-raising cookbook. This facsimile edition is an attempt to preserve those recipes and honor the 63 contributors -- many descendants of the HMS Mirlo rescuers.

Nothing is known of the book's history. We only know it was published after 1963 -- since there are Zip codes in some advertisements -- and before 1974, because one of the listed contributors, Bernice Ballance of Buxton, died that year at the age of 89. "Captain" Ballance was well known on the Outer Banks for holding the record catch of a 75-pound channel bass which he landed in the 1920s. The record stood for nearly 20 years.

The copy we used for this facsimile edition surfaced in Michigan when a friend's mother downsized her cookbook collection. She said she did not remember where she got it, probably at a library used-book sale.

Charity and community cookbooks, abbreviated CCB's by some scholars, had their beginning in 1864. That year a women's group in Philadelphia published *A Poetical Cook-Book* to raise money for a "sanitary fair" to aid soldiers fighting in the Civil War. It was an idea that caught on. Between then and the start of the First World War, 5,000 of them were published, chiefly by women's groups. The projects gave women the opportunity to learn organizational skills that they would use in many other endeavors, including the efforts to gain women the vote, fund charity organizations and support the prohibitionist movement. Food scholars regard the books as a vast untapped resource for the study of recipes and women's history.

In reality, what one finds in charity cookbooks are the recipes that were circulating in newspapers and magazines of their day. In older CCBs those can be interesting, but one can only use so many recipes for Jell-O, cheese and macaroni and "American" goulash. It is certain, though, that each one also contains at least a few priceless gems: family and local recipes that have been handed down through the generations. In many cases, these fund-raiser cookbooks are the only place those recipes exist outside the family recipe boxes and the notebooks that vanish as the generations roll on.

Hopefully this facsimile edition will keep alive the recipes and the memory of some of the heroic people of the North Carolina Outer Banks.

Recipes

COMPILED BY

Ladies' Auxiliary
Chicamacomico Banks Volunteer Fire Department
Rodanthe, North Carolina

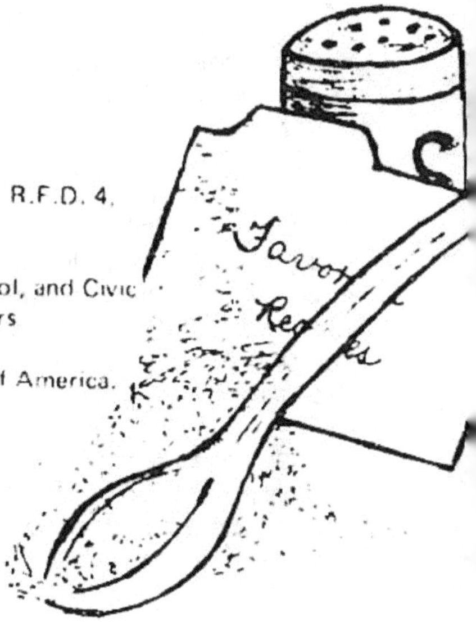

Walter's Publishing Company, R.F.D. 4,
Waseca, Minnesota 56093

Walter's serving Church, School, and Civic
Organizations for over 25 years

Printed in the United States of America.

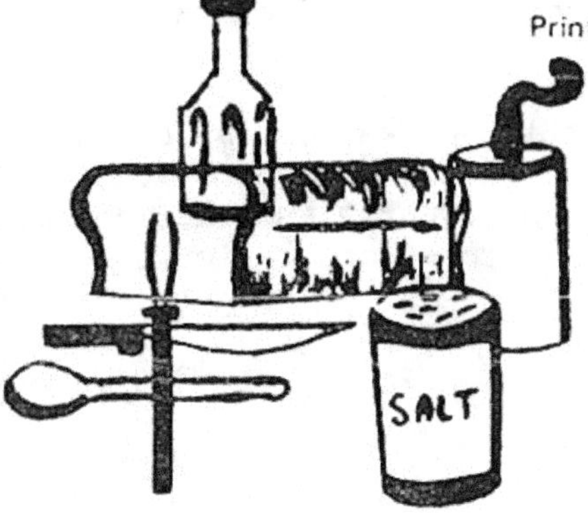

CHICAMACOMICO BANKS

Where is this area - or where was it? From whence came this name of lore and yore? Author David Stick's interesting book, "The Outer Banks of North Carolina", presents the answers.

But first, how does one pronounce this derivitive of a native Indian name? It's easy! Chic-a-ma-com-i-co. Accent "Chic" moderately, then pronounce each "a" in "a-ma" as in "ah" - low-key and long. Then really stress your accent on "com" and wind up with a fast but low-key "i-co". Chic-a-ma-COM-i-co. First, say it real slow. Repeat it, and then say it at normal speed, hitting that "COM" hard and the "i-co" fast. You'll never forget it!

The name first appeared in an official record of 1730. It was described as a 20-mile stretch of Hatteras Island from an inlet, now nonexistent but which then crossed the Pea Island Refuge, southward to Little Kinnakeet where you now see an old Lifesaving Station on the way down to Buxton. Actually, some pioneers had settled here nearly 30 years earlier.

Long before the Civil War, the live oak and cedar forests then here became highly desired timber for the famous clipper ships, so sand dunes gradually replaced the woodlands, and fishing became the primary, all-important means of livelihood.

During the Civil War, Confederate forces landed at the inlet and drove a Federal company camped here south to the point of the cape. Local residents fled with them, suffering extreme hardships on the long march, and their homes were ravished and burned. Federal regiments stationed at Hatteras then promptly chased the Confederate troops off the island. History books refer to this assail as the Chicamacomico Races!

Soon after the war, a Lifesaving Station and a Post Office were built in the northern village now known as Rodanthe. The Chicamacomico Banks Fire Department Station is located in Rodanthe and the Ladies Auxiliary is a division of this non-profit state corporation.

TABLE OF CONTENTS

	Page No.
BREAD AND ROLLS	1-8
MEATS, POULTRY	9-19
SEAFOODS	20-36
CANDIES, COOKIES	37-42
CAKES AND FROSTINGS	43-52
PIES, PASTRIES, DESSERTS	53-62
VEGETABLES	63-68
SALADS, MISCELLANEOUS	69-75
DIABETIC AND LOW CALORIE	76-81

FAVORITE RECIPES
FROM MY COOKBOOK

Recipe Name	Section	Page Number

BREAD & ROLLS

BANANA NUT BREAD   Donna Moher

1/3 c. shortening   1/2 tsp. soda
1/2 c. sugar   1/2 tsp. salt
2 eggs   1 c. mashed ripe bananas
1 3/4 c. sifted all-purpose flour 1/2 c. chopped walnuts or
1 tsp. baking powder   pecans

   Cream together shortening and sugar; add eggs and beat well. Sift together dry ingredients and add to creamed mixture alternately with bananas, blending well after each addition. Stir in nuts. Pour into well greased loaf pan. Bake in moderate oven (350o) for 45 to 50 minutes or until done when tested with a toothpick. Remove from pan, cool on rack, wrap and store overnight.

BEER MUFFINS   Joy Huggett

4 c. Bisquick   1 can of beer (room temperature)
2 tbsp. sugar

   Mix and fill greased muffin pans half full. Bake at 400° for 15 minutes.

EMILY'S FAMOUS BUTTERMILK BISCUITS   Soundside Restaurant

   Sift into large bowl or dishpan:
8 lbs. self-rising flour   1 tbsp. baking soda
   Add and mix by hand to fine crumbs:
1 lb. shortening
   Add and mix to a smooth dough:
1 1/2 gallons buttermilk
   Complete first three steps. Baking soda neutralizes buttermilk's acidity.
1/2 lb. flour and 3 c. butter
   Use 1/2 lb. flour to sprinkle over dough as you pinch and form biscuits. Place close together on greased and floured pans. Brush tops with melted butter; bake at 450° until golden brown. Yield: 148 biscuits (you are on your own to alter recipe.)

CHEESE BISCUITS
Frances Kapp

1 lb. grated sharp cheddar cheese (room temperature)
2 sticks oleo (room temperature)
2 c. flour
Dash of salt and garlic salt

Mix cheese and oleo well with mixer. Add flour and salts to this mixture. Make into small balls and refrigerate 20 minutes. Remove and bake on ungreased cookie sheet for 10 or 12 minutes at 425°.

LAURA'S BISCUITS
Laura Scarborough

2 c. flour
2 tsp. baking powder
1/2 to 2/3 tsp. salt as desired
Shortening size of egg or little larger
1/2 to 1 tsp. sugar to taste
Fresh milk or buttermilk

Put flour in sieve, add baking powder, salt and sugar. Sift ingredients twice. Add shortening and work with milk of choice. Roll out and cut and bake at 425-450° for 8-10 minutes.

LACY CORNBREAD
The Reef

1 c. white cornmeal
1 3/4 c. water
1 tbsp. salt (level)
Dash pepper
1 small onion, chopped fine

Mix all ingredients well. Drop from a tablespoon into 1/4 inch hot fat, allowing two tablespoons of batter to one corn cake. Brown well and turn to cook on other side, turning only once. Drain on paper towels. Makes approximately 2 dozen.

CORN BREAD
Janice Moher

1 c. corn meal
1 c. flour
1 c. evaporated milk
1 stick melted butter
1/4 c. sugar
4 tsp. baking powder
1 egg
Dash of salt

Mix in order; stir real good, and pour in greased pan and bake for 25 minutes at 350°.

CRANBERRY NUT BREAD
Ruth Frost

2 c. sifted flour
1 1/2 tsp. baking powder
1/2 tsp. soda
3/4 c. orange juice
1 c. chopped cranberries

1 c. sugar
1 tsp. salt
1/4 c. shortening
1 egg
1/2 c. chopped nuts

Sift together dry ingredients. Cut in shortening. Add juice and egg. Mix just to moisten. Fold in berries and nuts. Turn into greased loaf pan. Bake at 350° for 1 hour. Serve cool.

DATE NUT LOAF
Mrs. Asa Gray, Jr.

3/4 c. chopped walnuts
1 c. cut-up pitted dates
1 1/2 tsp. baking soda
1 tsp. vanilla flavoring
1 c. granulated sugar

1 1/2 c. sifted all-purpose flour
1/2 tsp. salt
3 tbsp. shortening
3/4 c. boiling water
2 eggs

Mix first 4 ingredients with fork. Add shortening, water. Let stand 20 minutes. Heat oven to 350°. Beat eggs with fork. Add date mixture, mixing to just blended. Pour into greased 9x5x3 inch loaf pan. Bake in moderate oven of 350° for 1 hour, 5 minutes or until done. Makes 1 loaf.

DILLY BREAD
Alys Conley

Mix 2 pkgs. dry yeast with 1/2 c. of warm water.
Heat 2 c. cottage cheese with 2 tsp. oleo until lukewarm. Then add 2 tsp. salt, 1/2 tsp. soda, 4 tsp. sugar, 2 tsp. instant onion, 4 tsp. dill seed and 2 beaten eggs. Add yeast and water to this mixture and then add 4 1/2 to 5 c. flour, or enough to make stiff dough. Mix well. Let rise until double. Stir down dough and divide into 2 well greased pans. Let rise 30 to 40 minutes. Bake at 350° for 40 to 50 minutes. Brush with soft butter when done.

GERMAN PANCAKES
Beverly Nobel

In blender, mix:
- 4 eggs
- 1 tbsp. sugar
- 1/3 c. milk
- 1 tbsp. oleo
- 1/3 c. flour

Pour 1/3 mixture on grill, lightly greased and cook until brown on both sides. Spread with butter or oleo, strawberry jam and roll up. Sprinkle confectioner's sugar on top. Yield: 3 cakes.

HUSH PUPPIES
Mellie Edwards

- 3/4 c. meal
- 1/4 c. flour
- 1 tsp. baking powder
- 1 tbsp. sugar
- 1/4 tsp. salt
- 1 small onion

Mix with milk to form ball. Drop into deep fat. I used this recipe for seven years in a restaurant.

ORANGE OATMEAL BREAD
Patricia Midgett

- 1 grated orange peel
- 6 tbsp. juice and pulp
- 2 tbsp. sugar (sprinkle over peel)
- 1 c. white flour
- 1/2 c. whole wheat flour
- 1/2 c. honey
- 4 1/2 tsp. baking powder
- 1/2 tsp. salt
- 1/4 tsp. baking soda
- 1 c. oats
- 2 eggs, beaten
- 2 tbsp. butter
- 2/3 c. water

Combine dry ingredients then combine wet ingredients. Mix both together for 10 minutes. Grease a 9x5 inch loaf pan and wax paper bottom and grease paper, too. Bake at 350° for 45 minutes to one hour or until a toothpick comes out clean.

PEANUT BUTTER PINEAPPLE LOAF BREAD
Joyce Midgett

- 2 1/4 c. flour
- 3/4 c. sugar
- 3 tsp. baking powder
- 1 tsp. salt
- 1/2 tsp. baking soda
- 1 c. bran cereal
- 2 beaten eggs
- 1 1/2 c. crushed pineapple, undrained
- 3 tbsp. peanut oil
- 1/2 c. peanut butter (CONT'D)

Peanut Butter Pineapple Loaf Bread (CONT'D)

Combine first 5 ingredients. Stir in remaining ingredients. Mix just enough to blend. Bake in greased loaf pan (9x5 inch) for 45 minutes at 350°.

PUMPKIN BREAD   Nedra Lutz

2/3 c. shortening   2 tsp. soda
2 2/3 c. sugar   1 1/2 tsp. salt
4 eggs   1/2 tsp. baking powder
1 lb. can pumpkin   1 tsp. cinnamon
2/3 c. water   1 tsp. cloves
3 1/3 c. flour   2/3 c. chopped nuts
                             2/3 c. raisins

Heat oven to 350°. Grease 2 loaf pans (9x5x3 inch). Cream shortening and sugar thoroughly. Add flour, eggs, pumpkin and water. Blend in dry ingredients except nuts and raisins, which are to be stirred in just before pouring into pans. Bake 65 to 75 minutes or until straw inserted in center comes out clean. Let cool in pans before removing. One may be wrapped in aluminum foil and frozen for future use.

PUMPKIN BREAD   Mrs. Asa Gray, Jr.

1 1/3 c. sugar   1 2/3 c. flour sifted with:
1/3 c. oil   1 tsp. soda
2 eggs   1/2 tsp. cloves
1 can pumpkin   3/4 tsp. salt
                               1/4 tsp. baking powder

Mix in order given and bake in greased bread pan at 325° for 1 hour and 10 minutes. Should be golden brown. NOTE: May take a little longer.

RAISIN BRAN MUFFINS   Kiki Caldwell

1 (15 oz.) box raisin bran   2 tsp. salt
2 c. sugar   4 eggs, beaten
5 c. flour   1 c. oil
2 tsp. soda   1 quart buttermilk

    Mix dry ingredients. Combine liquids and mix well with dry ingredients. (This will keep up to 6 weeks in an air tight container in the refrigerator.)
    To bake: put in greased muffin cups and bake at 400° for 15 to 20 minutes.

RUM ROLLS   Seafare Restaurant

2 c. milk   2 eggs
1 c. sugar   3 tsp. rum extract
1 c. shortening   7 c. flour
2 tsp. salt   4 tbsp. butter or margarine,
2 compressed yeast cakes   melted
                               1 c. seeded raisins, cut up

    Pour scalded milk over 1/2 c. sugar, shortening and salt. Cool to lukewarm and crumble yeast into it. Beat with rotary beater until smooth. Add beaten eggs and rum extract. Add 1/2 the flour and beat until smooth. Add remaining flour and beat until smooth. Cover with a clean towel and let rise in a warm place (80 to 85°) until double in bulk, about three hours. Roll dough into strips, each 12 inches long, 1/2 inch thick and 4 inches wide. Brush top with melted butter and sprinkle with sugar and raisins. Roll up, pulling dough out at the edges to keep uniform. Should be 15 inches long when rolled. Cut roll in cross-wise slices 3/4 inch thick. Place in 3 inch greased muffin tins, cover with a clean towel and let rise in a warm place until double in bulk. Bake in a moderately fast oven, 400° or 350° for 15 to 20 minutes. As soon as rolls are removed from oven cover with icing made with 2 c. confectioner's sugar, 4 tbsp. hot water, and 4 tsp. rum extract. Makes 36.

SCRIPTURE BREAD
Kiki Caldwell

3 c. flour	1 1/8 c. oil
1 1/2 tsp. salt	2 1/4 c. sugar
1 1/2 tsp. baking powder	1 1/2 tbsp. poppy seed
3 eggs	1 1/2 tbsp. each of almond,
1 1/2 c. milk	butter, and vanilla extract

Mix all together for 1 to 2 minutes. Pour into 2 greased loaf pans. Bake at 350° for one hour. Cool slightly. Poke holes in top with toothpick and pour glaze over top.

Glaze:

1/4 c. orange juice	1/2 tsp. each of almond, butter,
3/4 c. powdered sugar	and vanilla extract

WHOLE WHEAT BANANA BREAD
Sheree Covey

1/2 c. butter	1 tsp. soda
3/4 c. brown sugar	3/4 tsp. salt
1 egg	1/4 c. yogurt or buttermilk
1 c. unsifted whole wheat flour	1 1/4 c. mashed ripe bananas
1/2 c. unsifted white flour, unbleached	

Cream butter and sugar together until light and creamy. Beat in egg. Sift dry ingredients. Combine bananas and buttermilk. Stir to mix. Add dry ingredients with banana mixture, stir until combined well. Turn into a greased 9x5 inch loaf pan. Bake at 350° (preheat) for 50 to 60 minutes. Cool 10 minutes.

ZUCCHINI BREAD
Lee Warren

1 c. salad oil	3 c. all-purpose flour
3 eggs, slightly beaten	1 tsp. soda
2 c. sugar	1/4 tsp. baking powder
2 c. grated zucchini	1 tsp. salt
2 tsp. vanilla	3 tsp. ground cinnamon
1 c. chopped, black walnuts or pecans	

(CONT'D)

Zucchini Bread (CONT'D)

    Combine oil, eggs, sugar, zucchini, and vanilla in a large mixing bowl, blend well. Stir in flour, soda, baking powder, salt and cinnamon. Do not beat, stir in nuts. Spoon batter into well greased pans. Bake at 325° for 1 1/2 hours or until done.

MEATS, POULTRY

BARBECUE RIBS
                                                 Christi Dee Minor

Trim excess fat from about 4 lbs. lean pork spare ribs. Cut into serving size pieces (2 or 3 rib portions). Place into deep kettle and cover with cold water, add 1 tbsp. salt. Bring to boil and simmer 45 minutes. Remove from heat and drain in colander. Place ribs in shallow baking pan (pieces laid side by side trying not to overlap). Put two thin slices of onion on each piece. Cover each piece with barbecue sauce (below). Cook in oven 350° uncovered for 45 minutes. Serve hot.

Barbecue Sauce:
1 c. catsup
1 tbsp. vinegar
1 tbsp. brown sugar

1 c. water
1 tbsp. worcestershire sauce
Dash of pepper

Mix all ingredients thoroughly, spoon over ribs.

BEEF STROGANOFF
                                                 Warna Dale Gillies

1 lb. beef tenderloin
Seasoned flour
1/4 c. drawn butter
1/4 c. brandy
4 scallions, minced

6 parsley sprigs, minced
12 medium mushrooms, sliced
1 c. beef consomme
2 oz. Escoffier Diable or
    A-1 sauce
3/4 c. sour cream

Cut tenderloin in strips 2 inches long and 1/4 inch thick. Dip into seasoned flour. Put drawn butter in saute pan, heat until butter starts to brown. Add floured meat, cook until brown. Add brandy, scallions, mushrooms and parsley, cook 4 to 5 minutes. Add consomme, cook until thick. Add Diable sauce and sour cream. Remove from heat, serve immediately over hot buttered noodles. Serves 4.

BREAKFAST CASSEROLE
                                                 Mrs. Bethany M. Gray

1 lb. bulk pork sausage (hot or
    mild)
6 eggs
2 c. milk
1 tsp. dry mustard

1/2 tsp. salt
Dash of pepper
3 slices bread, cubed
1 c. shredded cheddar cheese

Crumble and saute sausage; drain. Beat eggs. Add milk and seasonings; beat together. Arrange bread cubes in pan. Top with sausage. Sprinkle on cheese. Pour egg mixture over all. Refrigerate overnight. Bake at 350° for 50-60 minutes, until puffy and brown.

BREAKFAST CASSEROLE   Jackie Pfost

6 slices bread, trimmed   1 lb. pork sausage, browned
1 tbsp. mustard   and drain
3 eggs   1 c. grated cheddar cheese
Dash: salt, pepper, nutmeg and   2 c. milk
      worcestershire

*Grease pan, line with bread, sausage, cheese, beat egg, milk and spices, pour over all. Bake at 350° (Check after 45 minutes, center should be done).

CAPE HATTERAS FRIED CHICKEN   Odessa Wasili

1 chicken fryer   1/2 tsp. paprika
1/2 c. vegetable oil   1/2 tsp. salt
1/2 c. pancake flour   1/4 tsp. black pepper

Wash chicken in cold water and cut into frying size pieces. Drain. Mix seasonings with pancake flour in paper bag. Heat oil in frying pan. Shake chicken parts in bag and fry until golden brown. Place in casserole or roasting pan, cover, and bake in preheated 350° oven for 30 minutes.

JAPANESE CHICKEN   Avis Turcotte

2 (2 1/2 lbs.) cut up chicken   1/2 c. water
1/4 c. flour   2 tbsp. red vinegar
4 tbsp. butter   1/4 c. brown sugar
1 1/2 tsp. ginger   1 can pineapple bits
1 small green pepper
1/4 c. soy sauce

Coat chicken with flour and ginger. Brown in butter. Mix remaining ingredients and pour over chicken.
Bake at 350° for 1 hour (30 minutes covered, 30 minutes uncovered). Serve with rice.

ROAST CHICKEN AND BISCUITS   Olive Patrick

1 frying chicken   1 can cream of chicken soup
Salt   1 can biscuits
Pepper

    Cut up chicken and prepare as for frying. Salt and pepper chicken and place in a roasting pan or a large fry pan which can be used in the oven. Add 1 can of cold water to the cream of chicken soup and mix well. Pour over chicken and cover. Cook in oven at 325° for about 1 1/2 hours or until tender. Add biscuits 20 minutes before chicken is done, after basting chicken. Raise oven heat to 450° for last 5 minutes to brown biscuits and leave pan uncovered.

CHICKEN RICE SURPRISE   Trisha Sandelli

6 medium chicken thighs   2 c. water
1 lb. can drained pineapple chunks 1 1/2 tsp. salt
1 c. uncooked rice   4 heaping tsp. flour

    Put just enough water in pan to cover chicken; put salt in water. Boil chicken till it loosens from bones. Drain and let cool. Prepare rice as on package. Pull chicken from bones in large chunks and place in 9x9x2 inch pan. Mix flour with 2 c. very hot water until smooth. Add to chicken. Heat on stove on low. Add rice and pineapple and mix together until lightly coated with sauce. Simmer until hot and serve. Serves 4 to 6.

    Possibilities to add: Fresh early peas (whole pods); or 8 oz. can drained corn.

CHICKEN AND RICE   Lennie Midgett

2 1/2 lbs. frying chicken   1/2 tsp. salt
1/2 c. rice   1/4 tsp. pepper

    Place rice in bottom of pan. Cut up chicken into serving pieces. Place on top of rice. Add salt and pepper and enough water to cover chicken. Boil over low heat for 45 minutes to 1 hour until chicken is tender.

CITY CHICKEN
Evelyn Seid

Put 2 lbs. boneless pork and/or veal, cut into 1 1/2 inch cubes on skewers or small popsicle sticks.
Mix together: 1 slightly beaten egg and 2 tbsp. milk.
Dip meat (on skewers) in this and roll in mixture of:

1/2 c. cracker crumbs (fine)	1/2 tsp. monosodium glutamate
1/2 c. corn flake crumbs	or thyme
1 tsp. paprika	Dash of pepper
3/4 tsp. poultry seasoning	

Brown slowly in 2 or 3 tbsp. of fat. Dissolve 1 chicken bouillon cube in 3/4 c. water and then pour on meat. Bake, covered, one hour (till tender) at 350°.

CALDWELL CLAN CHILI
The Caldwell Clan

2 lbs. lean ground beef, brown, drain and add:

2 tsp. (or more) chili powder	2 medium cans tomatoes
Dash or two of worcestershire sauce	1 large onion, chopped
1 large (53 oz.) can pork and beans	

Mix and cook covered on low heat 2 or 3 hours. Serve over cooked rice and sprinkle with grated cheddar cheese.

CHILI
Marilyn Davis

3 tbsp. butter or olive oil	1 tsp. cumin seed (crushed)
1 large onion (minced)	1 small bay leaf
2 cloves garlic (minced)	2 tbsp. chili powder
1 lb. hamburger	1/8 tsp. basil
2 c. V-8 juice	1 1/2 tsp. salt
1 large can stewed or canned tomatoes (undrained)	1 c. water
	1 small can tomato paste
1/2 tsp. celery seed	
1/4 tsp. cayenne pepper (red pepper)	

Saute onion and garlic in butter. Add meat and brown. Add remaining ingredients (all in large pot or dutch oven). Simmer uncovered 3 hours. Add 1 large can kidney beans (undrained) just before serving.

RED RIVER CHILI — Avis Turcotte

3 lbs. stewing beef	1 can green chili peppers
4 tbsp. oil	(4 oz.) seeded and diced
1 large onion, finely chopped	1 tsp. celery seed, crushed
1 clove garlic, minced	1 tsp. cumin seed, crushed
1 can tomatoes (2 lbs., 3 oz.)	1 tbsp. chili powder
1 can beef broth (13 3/4 oz.)	1 tsp. salt
2 cans (16 oz.) red kidney beans, drained	

Cut beef in 1/2 inch cubes. Brown part at a time in 2 tbsp. oil in large kettle or dutch oven. Remove as they brown.

Saute onion and garlic in remaining 2 tbsp. oil about 3 minutes.

Return beef to kettle. Add tomatoes, beef broth, chili peppers, celery and cumin seeds, chili powder and salt. Bring to boil then lower heat. Simmer, stirring occasionally for about 2 1/2 hours.

Add kidney beans, cook 15 minutes longer.

Serve over rice with shredded cheddar cheese, sour cream or chopped onions, if you wish.

HAMBURGER STEW — Louelle Midgett

1 lb. lean ground meat	3 large carrots
6 potatoes	3 pieces celery
3 onions	1 bouillon cube
1 can tomatoes	

Cook meat until lightly browned. Drop in carrots, celery, onions, tomatoes, bouillon cube. When carrots are almost done, drop in potatoes. Cook until done. Add little water to make gravy.

HAMBURGER TREAT — Mary Watson

1 lb. hamburger meat	1 1/2 c. catsup and water (mix together)
6 slices American cheese	Salt and pepper to taste
1 onion, sliced	

Make 6 hamburger patties, place in baking dish. Salt and pepper, 1 cheese slice on top of each pattie. Pour catsup mixed with water over top, add onions. Bake at 325° for approximately 35 to 45 minutes. Serve over toast.

HAM LOAF
Evelyn Seid

1 1/2 lbs. ground ham
1 1/2 lbs. ground pork
2 eggs, slightly beaten
2 tsp. worcestershire sauce
4 c. Rice Krispies
2 c. milk

Mix above together, shape into 2 small loaves. Bake at 350° for 2 hours. Last 1/2 hour, pour sauce over loaves and bake uncovered.

Sauce:
Mix together 1/2 c. brown sugar, 1 tsp. dry mustard and 2 tbsp. vinegar.

RAISIN SAUCE FOR HAM
Zenovah Hooper

1/2 c. brown sugar
1 tbsp. dry mustard
1/2 tbsp. flour
1/2 tsp. salt
1/8 tsp. pepper
1/4 c. vinegar
1/4 tsp. cloves
Few grains mace, nutmeg and cinnamon
1/2 c. seedless raisins
1 1/2 c. water

Mix dry ingredients. Add vinegar and water. Cook to a syrup. Serve hot. May be reheated.

HOT DOG CHILI
Georgia Simons

1 lb. hamburger, crumbled but not browned
1 pint of water

Combine and heat until hot and melted. Add:

1 c. ketchup
1 tsp. mustard
Salt and pepper to taste and chili powder

Cook slowly for about 1 hour.

MEAT LOAF
Mrs. Julian L. Gray

1 1/2 lbs. ground chuck
1 egg, beaten
1 1/2 tsp. salt
1 c. fresh bread crumbs
1 medium onion, chopped
1/4 tsp. pepper
1 can tomato sauce, small

Lightly mix ingredients and form a loaf. Place in shallow pan in moderate oven, 350°. While it's starting to bake, combine the following to make a Tart Sweet Sauce: (CONT'D)

Meat Loaf (CONT'D)

1/2 can tomato sauce
2 tbsp. brown sugar or molasses
2 tbsp. prepared mustard
2 tbsp. vinegar
1 c. water

    Pour over meat loaf in oven. Continue baking 1 1/2 hours longer, basting occasionally.

MEAT LOAF   Olive Patrick

2 1/2 lbs. ground beef
1 medium onion, diced
Salt
Pepper
1 can tomato soup
6 saltine crackers
3 cold biscuits or bread
2 eggs

    Mix ground beef, eggs, onion, salt, pepper, crackers, and bread crumbs with one half can of tomato soup. Turn into greased loaf or baking pan and cook in oven at 350°. After 30 minutes of cooking, drain grease off and pour remainder of tomato soup over top and continue cooking until done, a total of about 45 minutes.

OLD TIME STUFFED PEPPERS   Sheree Covey

6-8 green peppers
1 lb. ground beef
1/4 c. chopped onion
1 (12 oz.) can whole kernel corn,
    drained
1 c. tomato sauce
1 1/2 tsp. worcestershire
1/2 tsp. salt
4 oz. American cheese (shredded)
1/4 c. soft bread crumbs
2 tsp. margarine, melted

    Cut off tops of peppers, remove membranes. Precook peppers in 2 quarts of boiling water for about 5 minutes, drain. In skillet, brown meat and onion. Add corn, tomato sauce, worcestershire and salt. Simmer until heated through, about 5 minutes. Add cheese and stir until melted.
    Stuff peppers and stand upright in 12x7 1/2x2 inch baking dish. Combine bread crumbs and melted butter, sprinkle crumbs over tops of peppers. Fill baking pan 1/2 inch water. Bake at 350° (uncovered) for 35 to 40 minutes.

BARBECUED PORK CHOPS   Olive Patrick

8 lean pork chops   1/2 tsp. nutmeg
1/2 c. catsup   1/3 c. vinegar
1 tsp. salt   1 c. water
1 tsp. celery seed   1 bay leaf

   Brown chops in hot fat. Combine remaining ingredients. Pour over chops. Bake in slow oven (325°) for 1 1/2 hours. Turn chops once during baking. Makes 8 servings.

SAUSAGE STUFFING   Joan Berry

2 loaves stale bread   Poultry seasoning, 2 to 3
4-5 stalks celery (chopped)   tsp. as desired
1 large onion (chopped)   Salt
1 lb. bulk pork sausage   Pepper
4 eggs   Milk

   Cook celery, onion and sausage in frying pan. Add to bread that has been broken up into small pieces. Add eggs, poultry seasoning, salt and pepper, and mix. Add milk until mixture is very moist. This will make enough dressing to stuff a 15-20 lb. turkey.

ITALIAN SPAGHETTI SAUCE   Laura Scarborough

1 big onion, chopped fine   1 tbsp. worcestershire sauce
1 garlic clove, chopped fine   1 tbsp. dry mustard
1 bell pepper, chopped fine   1 tbsp. sugar
1 1/2 lbs. hamburger   1 tsp. hot sauce
1 oz. olive oil   1 tbsp. oregano
1 small can tomatoes   Salt and pepper as desired
1 heaping tbsp. chile powder   1/2 c. red wine (optional)
1 can tomato paste

   Heat olive oil in large dutch oven or skillet. Add onion, garlic, bell pepper and hamburger. Simmer 30 minutes stirring often. Add tomatoes, tomato paste and 3 cans of water. Add chile powder, oregano, hot sauce, worcestershire sauce, mustard, sugar, salt and pepper. Cook slowly for 2 or 3 hours or longer, stirring occasionally. Add wine 30 minutes before done. Serve hot over spaghetti.

                                                          (CONT'D)

Italian Spaghetti Sauce (CONT'D)

Spaghetti:
Boil 1 lb. package of spaghetti in 2 quarts salted water until tender. Drain off water, add 1/3 stick of butter or margarine to melt over spaghetti. Sift on grated cheese. For better flavor add sauce to spaghetti in individual plates.

QUICK SPAGHETTI   Louelle Midgett

1 lb. hamburger   2 cans tomato sauce
1 can tomatoes   1 small onion
1 tsp. garlic salt   Pepper to taste

Cook hamburger until lightly browned, pour in tomato sauce, add onion in small pieces, garlic salt, pinch chili powder. Simmer for half hour. Add enough water to add spaghetti in same pot.

QUICK SPAGHETTI SAUCE   Cleve Webber

2 pkgs. Lipton onion soup   1 large can tomato paste
2 cans tomatoes   1 lb. hamburger

Saute hamburger in pot you will use, until it is completely crumbled. Add above ingredients plus enough water to boil briskly for 1/2 hour. Add chili powder when variety is desired. This recipe cooked to desired thickness also makes a good "sloppy joe".

QUICHE LORRAINE   Marilyn Davis

2 (9 inch) pie shells, baked 5 minutes at 450°.
8 strips bacon (fried crisp)   2 c. table cream
1 large onion, thinly sliced   1/4 tsp. nutmeg
2 c. swiss cheese (cubed)   1/2 tsp. salt
1/2 c. parmesan cheese   1/4 tsp. pepper
4 eggs, lightly beaten   Dash of garlic powder

Saute onion until transparent, using 1 tbsp. bacon fat. Crumble the bacon and sprinkle the bacon, onion and cheese over inside of the partly baked pastry shells. Combine the eggs, cream, nutmeg, salt and pepper, and strain over the onion/cheese mixture.

Bake at 450° for 15 minutes. Reduce the temperature to 350° and bake 10 minutes longer. Serve immediately.

ROAST DUCK WITH HONEY GLAZE — Lucretia Midgett

Clean duck, rub inside and out with salt and pepper, do not prick skin. Stuff with favorite dressing (optional). Place breast side up on rack in roasting pan. Do not add water. Roast uncovered in shallow pan in slow oven (325°), 1 1/2 to 2 hours for moderately done, 2 to 2 1/2 hours for well done, meaty part of leg should feel tender. Thirty minutes before duck is done, brush with honey glaze containing 2 tbsp. honey and 1 tsp. kitchen bouquet.

SAUSAGE BALLS — Marilyn Davis

Mix together well:
- 2 c. Bisquick
- 1 lb. hot sausage (bulk roll)
- 2 c. grated sharp cheese (NOTE: Grate your own cheese. Cheese bought already grated is too dry).

Form balls about the size of walnuts. Bake at 350° for 15 to 20 minutes.

TAMALE LOAF — Marie Fagundes

- 1/2 c. salad oil
- 3 tbsp. butter
- 2 onions, minced
- 2 cloves garlic, minced
- 1 (#303) can tomatoes
- 1 (#303) can corn
- 3 tbsp. chili powder dissolved in small amount of water
- 1 1/2 c. corn meal
- 3 eggs, beaten
- 1 c. milk
- 1 1/2 c. black pitted olives
- 1 tbsp. salt
- 1 c. hamburger (browned) or diced cooked ham

In a large skillet, cook onion and garlic in oil and butter until onions are transparent. Add all other ingredients in order given and cook 15 minutes more. Stir continuously to avoid sticking to skillet. Pour into baking dish and bake at 350° for 30 minutes or until firm.

SANDELLI'S ZUCCHINI Trisha Sandelli

4 (8 to 10 inch) zucchini
1 lb. ground beef
1 brick mild Colby cheese
1 c. grated mozzarella cheese
Garlic salt, salt and pepper

    Blanch zucchini, remove and pat dry. Slice zucchini longways and scoop middle out and place in a baking pan. Place meat in skillet and brown lightly. Spoon meat into zucchini shells. Sprinkle garlic salt onto meat; sprinkle mozzarella cheese next. Slice Colby cheese into narrow strips. Criss-cross on top lengthwise across whole shell and meat. Lightly sprinkle with salt and pepper. Bake in preheated oven at 350° for 20 minutes or until' skin of shell is soft and cheese is melted. Serves 8.
    Serves nicely with lightly buttered and garlic powdered garlic bread.

SEAFOODS

BLUEFISH WITH BARBECUE SAUCE
Avis Turcotte

2 (2 lbs. each) split and
    dressed bluefish
3 tbsp. oil
1 clove garlic, crushed
2 tbsp. finely chopped green onions
1 tbsp. soy sauce

1/3 c. catsup
2 tbsp. orange juice
1/4 tsp. pepper
1/8 tsp. leaf oregano, crumbled

    Preheat broiler. Place fish, skin side down, on well greased broiler rack. Combine all other ingredients and spoon mixture over fish. Place broiler so top of fish is 2 inches from heat. Broil 8 minutes or until fish flakes easily. Serves 6-8.

BLUEFISH SNACK
W. J. Midgett

3 to 4 c. water
1/3 c. horseradish
3 tbsp. crushed red pepper

Juice from 1/2 lemon
4 lbs. bluefish

    Combine all ingredients except bluefish. Bring to a boil. Cut fish into 3 inch by 1 inch pieces and drop into boiling mixture. Boil 8 minutes. Remove from heat and drain. Serve hot or cold with melted butter.

BOILED BLUE FISH
Mrs. Asa Gray, Jr.

1 fish (medium size)
1 potato (medium size)

4 slices bacon
Salt

    Put peeled potato in pot with just enough water to cover the potato. Cook 10 minutes, add fish. Boil for 5 minutes, add salt. Cook 4 strips of bacon. Remove fish and potatoes from water. Pepper well if desired. Pour bacon drippings over fish and potatoes.
    Very good served with green salad and hush puppies.

STEAMED CLAMS
Olive Patrick

Thoroughly scrub 2 dozen clams in shell. Place in kettle with 1 c. hot water. Cover tightly and cook over medium heat just until shells open, about 10 minutes. Pour clam liquor into separate dish. Serve clams with melted butter. Makes 4 to 6 servings.

CLAMS CASINO
Marilyn Davis

2 dozen small fresh clams, open on half shell (reserve juice if possible)
1/2 c. chopped onion (chop fine)
1/2 c. chopped green pepper (chop fine)
Garlic salt
Lemon juice
Salt and pepper to taste
8 strips bacon, cut in thirds

Sprinkle clams with onion, green pepper, garlic salt, pepper, salt, and lemon juice. Top each with 1/3 bacon strip and broil 3 to 5 minutes, until bacon is crisp. Serve immediately.

CLAMS CASINO
Mrs. Reba Midgett

1 dozen large clams, minced
2 medium onions, minced
2 small bell peppers, minced
6 strips of bacon
Salt and pepper to taste
Parmesan cheese, if desired

Open clams, save shells. Put a layer of minced clams, a layer of onion and bell pepper in washed shell with salt and pepper to taste. Put part of bacon strip on top, sprinkle with parmesan cheese if desired. Bake in preheated oven at $400°$ until done, approximately 20 minutes.

CLAM FRITTERS
Dorcas Midgett

1 quart clams (well washed and drained)
2 eggs
1/2 c. flour
1/2 tsp. salt
1/2 tsp. pepper
1/2 tsp. baking powder

Chop clams rather fine, stir in eggs, flour, salt, pepper, and baking powder, mix well. Drop by tablespoonfuls into hot grease in skillet and fry until brown on both sides.

QUICK CRAB BISQUE
                                        Emily Landrum

1 stick butter   1 tsp. white pepper
1/2 c. flour   1 tsp. salt
1 pint half and half   1/4 tsp. nutmeg
2 c. milk   1 lb. crabmeat
1 small jar pimento, diced fine   1/2 c. dry sherry

Melt butter over low heat and stir in flour until smoothly blended. Stir constantly. Roux should bubble but not brown. Add half and half, milk, diced pimentos and seasoning. Continue stirring until thickened. Fold in crabmeat and heat through but do not boil. Add wine to mixture and simmer 5 more minutes. This should be a very thick soup. If too thick, milk may be added after crabmeat.

CRAB BISQUE
                                        Linda Hooper

Melt one stick of butter in a saucepan. Add 2 tbsp. cornstarch, 3-4 c. milk, salt, pepper, hot sauce (if desired), 2 c. crabmeat. Simmer for about 10-15 minutes.

CRAB CAKES
                                        Witty Donahoe Minton

1 lb. crab meat   1 tbsp. mayonnaise
2 eggs, well beaten   1 tsp. salt
1 small onion, chopped   Pepper to taste
2 tbsp. prepared mustard   1 c. mashed potatoes

Mix all. Make into cakes and fry.

CRAB CAKES
                                        Linda Hooper

2 c. crab meat   1/4 c. flour
2 eggs   1 tsp. Texas Pete Hot Sauce
1/2 c. cracker crumbs

Mix all ingredients, form into patties and fry in hot grease.

CRAB IN CHAFING DISH
Witty Donahoe Minton

2 lbs. backfin crab meat
1 1/2 c. mayonnaise
1 small bottle Durkees sauce (<u>no</u> substitutes)
Season to taste with: paprika, hot pepper sauce, salt and worcestershire sauce

Combine ingredients. Mix gently but well. Heat and serve with Melba rounds. Excellent at Coffees', Teas' and Cocktail Parties.

DEVILED CRAB
Louelle Midgett

1 lb. crab meat
1 can She Crab soup
Pepper and salt to taste
1 egg, beaten
Seafood seasoning to taste

Mix together. Pack in cleaned crab shells. Broil in oven until browned.

DEVILED CRAB
Linda Hooper

2 c. crabmeat
2 tbsp. mayonnaise
1 tbsp. Durkee famous sauce
1 tbsp. worcestershire sauce
Cracker crumbs and butter
1 tsp. Texas Pete sauce

Mix crab meat with mayonnaise, Durkee Sauce, worcestershire sauce and Texas Pete Hot sauce. Put in crab shells. Top with cracker crumbs and butter. Bake at 350° for 20 minutes.

HOT CRAB DIP
Witty Donahoe Minton

1 pkg. (8 oz.) cream cheese, softened
8 oz. crab meat
2 tbsp. chopped onion
1 tbsp. milk
1/2 tsp. prepared horseradish
1/4 tsp. salt
Dash pepper
1 c. toasted sliced almonds

Combine all except nuts. Blend well. Spoon into ovenproof dish. Sprinkle with almonds. Bake in 375° oven for 15 minutes. Transfer to chafing dish and keep warm. Serve with toast points or crackers.

LOUISIANA CRAB GUMBO   Karl Baarslag

1 lb. of claw or flake crab meat, fresh or frozen
3/4 lb. cooked and deveined cut up shrimp, preferably fresh
3 tbsp. butter, oleo, olive oil or cooking oil, to suit taste
3 tbsp. flour
2 medium onions, minced very fine
2 large ripe tomatoes, (canned tomatoes may be used)
1 quart of water
1/4 tsp. of powdered garlic or 1 minced garlic
1 quart milk (for a thicker gumbo cut down water and use 1/2 pint of half and half)
2 to 3 dashes of paprika according to taste
1 tsp. parsley
4 bay leaves
Salt to taste, or omit for salt free diet

Melt butter in a large deep skillet, sprinkle in flour until well mixed, add minced onions and let simmer until onion turns golden. Add the crab meat, shrimp cut into small pieces, and the water and milk and cook over a low fire for 45 to 50 minutes. Add the minced tomatoes and all seasoning and let simmer over low fire for 15 minutes. DO NOT BOIL.

CRAB IMPERIAL   Myrna Peters

3 tbsp. flour
3 tbsp. butter
1 c. milk
1 c. mayonnaise
1 tbsp. worcestershire sauce
1/2 tsp. salt
1/8 tsp. Tabasco sauce
1 egg, well beaten
1 1/2 lbs. back fin-blue crab meat

Melt butter, blend in flour, then add milk, and cook, stirring until thick. Cool. Blend in mayonnaise and seasonings. Fold in egg, then gently fold in crabmeat. Spoon into individual crab shells or casseroles. Sprinkle with paprika and bake at 400° for 10-12 minutes or until bubbly. Serves 6.

HOT CRAB SALAD
Witty Donahoe Minton

3 tbsp. oleo
1/2 c. chopped onion
1/2 green pepper, chopped
3 large celery ribs, chopped
    Cook the above in oleo and add:
2 c. tiny noodles, cooked (1 3/4 c.)

2 c. mayonnaise
2 c. chopped shrimp
2 c. crab meat
1 tbsp. lemon juice
1/2 tbsp. worcestershire sauce
1/2 tsp. salt

    Mix. Pour into greased casserole. Bake at 400° for 20 minutes.

CRAB STUFFING
Myrna Peters

1 lb. crab meat
1/2 c. onion, chopped
1/3 c. celery, chopped
1/3 c. green peppers, chopped
1 clove garlic, chopped
1/3 c. cooking oil

2 c. bread cubes
3 eggs, beaten
1 tbsp. parsley, chopped
2 tsp. salt
Pepper to taste

    Drain crab meat. Cook onions, celery, green peppers and garlic in cooking oil until tender. Combine with other ingredients and mix. Use for stuffing fish, shrimp, lobster, or other seafood.

FILLETS IN FOIL CHARCOAL-GRILLED
Myrna Peters

King fish-or any large fish, cut into fillets
2 lbs. fillets
2 green peppers, sliced
2 onions, sliced
1/4 c. melted butter

2 tbsp. lemon juice
2 tsp. salt
1 tsp. paprika
Black pepper to taste

    Cut fillets into serving pieces. Cut aluminum foil about 1 foot square and grease lightly. Place fillets, skin down, on foil. Top with green pepper and onions. Make sauce out of remaining ingredients and pour over fish. Wrap lightly in foil and grill about five inches from well-seasoned firebed for 45 to 60 minutes or until fish flakes.

PARMESAN ROLLED FILLETS
Avis Turcotte

6 flounder or perch fillets
1/3 c. butter or margarine
2 tbsp. lemon juice
1/4 tsp. paprika
1/2 tsp. onion salt
1/4 tsp. pepper

2 tbsp. butter or margarine
1 c. soft bread crumbs (2 slices)
2 tbsp. grated parmesan cheese

Roll each fillet starting with tail end. Place in greased shallow baking dish. Preheat broiler. Melt 1/3 c. butter or oleo; add lemon juice, paprika, onion salt and pepper. Spoon 1/2 over fillets. Melt 2 tbsp. butter or oleo, combine with bread crumbs and parmesan cheese. Place fillets in broiler about 3 inches from heat. Broil 5 minutes. Turn carefully. Spoon over remaining butter mixture. Sprinkle with cheese-crumb mixture. Turn broiler heat down halfway - broil 1-2 minutes until crumbs are browned. 6 servings.

BAKED PARMESAN FILLETS
Bette R. Gray

1 c. cornflake crumbs
3/4 c. (3 oz.) grated cheddar cheese (mild), or Parmesan
1/2 tsp. salt

2 lbs. fish fillets
2 eggs, slightly beaten
2 tbsp. milk

Combine crumbs, cheese and salt. Dip fillets in combined egg and milk; coat with crumb mixture. Place in greased 13x9 inch pan. Bake at 450° for 20 minutes or until fish flakes easily with fork. 6 servings.

FISH CHOWDER
Debi Hooper

1 lb. cooked fish
3 cans mushroom soup
2 cans asparagus soup
1 can cream of shrimp soup
1/2 c. white wine
2 green peppers (chopped)

1 large onion, chopped
2 sticks butter
1/2 c. flour
1/2 gallon milk
1/2 tsp. each of season salt, garlic salt, parsley, salt and pepper

(CONT'D)

Fish Chowder (CONT'D)

Melt one stick of the butter and add onion and green pepper and cook til tender. Add soups and milk, wine and fish. Cook on low heat. Melt other stick of butter and add flour to it to make a roux. Add to Chowder and stir till thick.

FISH AND VEGETABLES   Bruce D. Midgett

1/2 large zucchini squash   4 small potatoes, sliced round
2 c. picked fish   2 handfulls grapes, fresh
                                      picked

Lightly brown fish and potatoes. Add 1 c. water. Put zucchini and grapes under potatoes and fish. Cover and simmer on medium heat for 15 to 21 minutes. Ready to eat.

FISH AND ZUCCHINI   George Chervenak

2 to 3 lbs. skinned fish   1 large onion, sliced
6 or 7 slices bacon   1 jar Ragu or any spaghetti
1 or 2 medium zucchini (1/4 to   sauce
   3/8 inch rounds)   Mozzarella cheese (shredded)

Fry bacon but not well done. Place strips and fat in bottom of roaster. Place fish on top of bacon. Place onion and zucchini on top of fish and pour spaghetti sauce over all. Sprinkle on cheese. Cover and cook in oven one hour at 350°. This recipe excellent with Puppy Drum and King Mackeral.

ESCALLOPED OYSTERS   Marie Fagundes

1/2 c. butter or margarine   4 tbsp. onion, chopped
3/4 c. flour   4 tbsp. green pepper, chopped
3 tsp. paprika   1/2 tsp. garlic, chopped
1 tsp. salt   2 tsp. lemon juice
1/2 tsp. black pepper   1 tbsp. worcestershire sauce
2 tbsp. cracker crumbs   1 quart oysters

Melt butter, add flour and cook for 5 minutes or until dark brown. Stir constantly. Add paprika, salt, black pepper, cook for 3 minutes.   (CONT'D)

Escalloped Oysters (CONT'D)

    Add onion, green pepper and garlic (which has been finely chopped), cook slowly for 5 minutes. Take from fire and add lemon juice, worcestershire sauce and oysters, (which have been picked over and heated in own liquor). Pour into baking dish, sprinkle cracker crumbs over the top. Bake in oven at 400° for 30 minutes.

SCALLOPED OYSTERS   Nina M. Minor

2 quarts fresh oysters   1 tbsp. lemon juice
1 tsp. salt   1 lb. saltine crackers
1/2 tsp. pepper   3 tbsp. butter, melted
1 tbsp. worcestershire sauce

    Preheat oven to 375°. Grease a 2 quart casserole. Season oysters with salt, pepper, worcestershire sauce and lemon juice. Coarsely crumble the crackers. Line bottom of casserole with a layer of crackers then a layer of oysters and repeat procedure, finishing with crackers. Sprinkle butter on top layer of crackers. Bake at 375° for 20 minutes.

OYSTER PIE   Alys Conley

1 pint of oysters   3 eggs
4 c. Ritz crackers   1/2 tsp. salt
1/4 lb. butter, melted   Dash of pepper
2 c. milk

    Grease a 9 or 10 inch baking dish (2 1/2 inches deep). Using about 1/4 of the cracker crumbs, spread a layer on the bottom of the dish. Place oysters close together and put remaining crumbs on top. Mix eggs, milk, butter, salt and pepper together and pour over crumbs. Bake at 325° for 30 minutes, or till the consistency of custard.

PUPPY DRUM STEW   Joan Berry

5-7 lbs. Puppy Drum   6-7 carrots
Salt pork or bacon   2 medium onions
6-7 medium potatoes   1 can Cream of Celery soup

    Clean fish, and cut into serving size pieces.   (CONT'D)

Puppy Drum Stew (CONT'D)

    Melt down salt pork or pieces of bacon in bottom of dutch oven. Layer fish, thickly sliced potatoes, thinly sliced carrots, and sliced onions. Repeat with another layer of each. Pour can of soup over the layers. Cook over medium heat until vegetables are done, approximately 45 minutes to one hour.

SALMON LOAF   Joan Berry

1 can (16 oz.) salmon
1 can condensed cream of celery soup
1 c. fine dry bread crumbs
2 eggs, slightly beaten
1/2 c. onion, chopped
1 tbsp. lemon juice

    Drain salmon, save 1/4 c. liquid. Remove skin and bones; flake. Thoroughly mix with salmon liquid and other ingredients. Pack into a well greased loaf pan. Mixture will be soft before baking. Bake at 375° for 1 hour (until browned). Cool 10 minutes in pan before removing.

SALMON LOAF WITH SHRIMP SAUCE   Marie Fagundes

2 (1 lb.) cans salmon or boiled skinless fish fillets
1/4 c. finely minced onion
1/4 c. chopped parsley
1/4 c. lemon juice
1/2 tsp. salt
1/2 tsp. pepper
1/2 tsp. ground thyme
2 c. coarse cracker crumbs
About 1/2 c. milk
4 eggs, well beaten
1/4 c. butter, melted

    Drain salmon, saving liquid. Flake salmon or fish fillets into bowl; add onion, parsley, lemon juice, seasonings and cracker crumbs; mix lightly. Add salmon liquid or liquid from boiled fish plus enough milk to make 1 cup; add eggs and melted butter. Mix lightly. Spoon into greased 2 quart loaf pan or casserole. Bake in moderate oven (350°) for 1 hour or until loaf is set in center. Makes 8 servings.

    <u>Shrimp Sauce:</u> Heat a can of frozen condensed cream of shrimp soup according to directions on label. Add 1/4 c. milk, stir until smooth. Spoon onto hot salmon loaf. OR you may substitute 1 1/2 c. white sauce to which 3/4 c. chopped steamed shrimp has been added.

SCALLOPS MORNAY
Mrs. Joye Krauel

2 lbs. scallops
White wine to cover
Sauce Mornay
Buttered crumbs
Grated Parmesan cheese

Poach the scallops in white wine for 3 to 5 minutes, until they are just cooked. Drain them and use the drained liquid to prepare the sauce Mornay. Arrange the scallops in a flat dish and cover with the sauce. Sprinkle with the buttered crumbs and a little grated parmesan cheese. Heat under the broiler for a few minutes to brown the top.

Sauce Mornay:
2 tbsp. flour
2 tbsp. butter or margarine
1 c. liquid from scallops
Salt and pepper to taste

Combine the flour and butter and cook together until they are slightly browned or yellowish in color. Gradually stir in the fish liquid and continue stirring until it thickens. Simmer 10 minutes and season to taste. Add 1/2 c. Parmesan cheese (grated) and stir. Can be doubled for more sauce on the scallops.

BAKED SEAFOOD CASSEROLE
Witty Donahoe Minton

1 lb. crab meat
1 lb. shrimp
1 c. mayonnaise
1/2 c. chopped green pepper
1/4 c. chopped celery
1/2 tsp. salt
1 tbsp. worcestershire sauce
Paprika

Combine all and sprinkle with paprika. Bake at 400° for 20 minutes.

BAKED SHAD
Janice Moher

1 Shad
Salt and pepper
4 slices bacon
1 large onion, sliced

Salt and pepper fish. Put bacon and onions on top of fish and wrap in aluminum foil. Bake in 250° oven for 5 hours.

SHRIMP CASSEROLE
W.J. Midgett

1/2 c. chopped onion	3 tbsp. flour
1/2 c. chopped green peppers	Salt and pepper to taste
1/2 c. chopped celery	1/2 c. milk or cream
3 tbsp. butter	2 lbs. cleaned chopped shrimp

Make a white sauce of butter, flour, milk and seasons. Stir in rest of ingredients. Pour into greased casserole, bake at 350° for 30 to 40 minutes.

ALMA WORKMAN'S SHRIMP DIP
Georgia Simons

1 (4 1/2 oz.) can shrimp, drained and shredded with fork until very fine
1 medium grated onion
1 1/2 c. grated sharp cheddar cheese
1 c. mayonnaise (or enough to make consistency of dip)

FRENCH FRIED SHRIMP
Sandy Kierzkowski

1 c. plain flour	2 tbsp. salad oil
1/2 tsp. sugar	2 lbs. deveined, shelled, raw shrimp
1/2 tsp. salt	
1 egg	Oil for deep fat frying
1 c. ice water	

Combine flour, salt, sugar, egg, ice water and 2 tbsp. salad oil. Beat thoroughly. Add shrimp. Stir to coat well. Heat oil until very hot. Using fork, lift shrimp one by one from batter. Drop in hot oil. Fry until golden (about 5 minutes). Drain on paper towels. Serves 6.

SHRIMP GUMBO
Mrs. Keith Fearing, Jr.

1 lb. raw shrimp, shell and devein	2 cans (1 lb., 3 oz.) tomatoes
3 tbsp. oleo	3 chicken flavored bouillon cubes
3/4 c. chopped onion	
3/4 c. chopped green pepper	3 c. boiling water
3/4 c. celery, sliced thin	1 1/2 tsp. salt
1 clove minced garlic or powder	1/2 tsp. pepper
2 pkgs. (10 oz.) frozen sliced okra	1/2 tsp. thyme leaves or powder
	3 bay leaves

(CONT'D)

Shrimp Gumbo (CONT'D)

Melt oleo in large saucepan. Saute' next four ingredients until soft. Chop tomatoes. Dissolve bouillon cubes in the boiling water. Add okra, tomatoes, bouillon mix and seasonings into the sauteed vegetables. Bring just to a boil and cover. Simmer about 30 minutes. Stir in shrimp and cook about 3 minutes. DO NOT OVERCOOK THE SHRIMP.

SHRIMP SUPREME   Florence Daley

1 medium onion (thinly sliced)   24 Jumbo shrimp
1 stalk celery (thinly sliced)   1 oz. brandy
Butter (for saute' - small amount) 1/2 c. Doxsee clam juice

Place onions and celery in fry-pan with small amount of butter and saute' until they (onions) are transparent. (Do not brown). Add shelled, de-veined shrimp and saute' until they just begin to turn pink. Sprinkle brandy over shrimp and ignite. When flames subside, add clam juice and simmer for 5 minutes. Remove from heat and set aside.

Cream Sauce:

4 tbsp. butter   Salt and pepper (to taste)
6 tbsp. flour   1/2 c. small cubes cheddar
2 c. light cream   cheese (extra-sharp)
Pinch of basil

In saucepan: Make a roux with butter and flour. Slowly add cream to roux, stirring and mixing constantly. Remove from (low) heat occasionally if necessary, while stirring to maintain a smooth paste effect. Continue in this manner until all the cream has been added. Add basil and salt and pepper. Set aside.

When ready to serve: Combine shrimp mixture and Cream Sauce. Reheat gently (stirring frequently). When hot add cheddar cheese cubes, stir for two minutes and serve over hot toast points. Sprinkle with paprika.

Green Salad and a dry white wine go well with this recipe. D'Anjou Pears for dessert.

REGAL SHRIMP
Sandy Kierzkowski

2 lbs. shelled medium shrimp (uncooked)
2 tbsp. butter
1 c. chopped onion
1 c. chopped green pepper
1 can (10 1/2 oz.) condensed mushroom soup
1 c. sour cream
1/3 c. catsup
1 can (4 oz.) mushrooms, drained
1 tbsp. lemon juice
1/4 c. dry white wine

Season 3 quarts boiling water with salt and 1 tbsp. lemon juice. Add shrimp. Boil 3 minutes and drain. Melt butter in large skillet or electric casserole set at 350°. Add onions, green pepper and saute until onion is transparent. Add soup, sour cream, catsup, mushrooms, lemon juice, wine and cooked shrimp. Reduce temperature to 325°. Stir mixture and heat for 5 minutes. Serve over rice.

SHRIMP CONGEALED SALAD
Witty Donahoe Minton

1 1/2 tbsp. gelatin
1/2 c. cold water
1 can tomato soup, heated
2 small cream cheese
1/2 c. mayonnaise
1 c. chopped celery
3 c. cut shrimp
1 tbsp. minced onion
1/2 tsp. salt
Dash of red pepper

Soak gelatin in water. Add soup and cream cheese and cool. Add mayonnaise, celery, shrimp, onion, salt and red pepper. Pour in mold.

SHRIMP E'TOUFFEE (SMOTHERED SHRIMP)
Sandy Kierzkowski

3 lbs. shrimp (raw-shelled)
1 c. chopped onions
1/2 c. chopped celery
1/4 tsp. tomato paste
1/4 lb. oleo or 1/2 c. cooking oil
1 1/4 tsp. cornstarch
1/2 c. cold water
Salt, black pepper and red pepper (as desired)

Peel shrimp, season generously with salt, black and red pepper. Set aside. Melt oleo/oil, add onions, celery and tomato paste. Cook slowly in an uncovered heavy pot until onions are transparent.
(CONT'D)

Shrimp E-Touffee (CONT'D)

Dissolve cornstarch in cold water. Add to mixture.
    Add seasoned shrimp and cook over medium heat about 20 minutes. Serve with rice. Serves 6.

CHARCOAL-GRILLED SURFSIDE SPOT   Myrna Peters

Freshly Caught Spots   Minced parsley
Salt and black pepper to taste   Bacon strips, cut in half
Onion, chopped
    Dress spots, clean and dry on paper towels. Cut piece of aluminum foil for each fish. Grease foil lightly, (may be greased by rubbing bacon strips on foil.) Place fish in center of foil and sprinkle on salt, pepper, onions, and parsley. Top with strip of bacon. Fold foil around fish tightly and cook for 10 to 15 minutes, or until fish flakes when tested.
    NOTE: This is an all purpose recipe which works well with other small fish such as croaker, drum, or blue. For natural flavor leave out onion and parsley.

FIRST MATE'S STEW   Bette R. Gray

29 oz. can tomatoes   1 c. yellow squash slices
1 c. celery chunks   1/2 c. barbecue sauce
1 c. chopped onion   (better with hickory
1 c. green pepper chunks   flavor)
                                           1 tsp. salt
                                           1 lb. fish fillets, partially cut into 1 inch cubes or larger, flounder very good).
    Combine vegetables, barbecue sauce and salt in Dutch oven. Cover; simmer 20 minutes. Add fish to vegetable mixture. Cover; continue simmering 8 minutes or until fish flakes easily with fork, stirring occasionally. 6 servings.

BROILED TROUT
Sarah Midgett

2 lbs. skinless trout fillets
    or other fresh fillets
2 tbsp. onion, grated
1 1/2 tsp. salt
1/8 tsp. pepper

2 large tomatoes, cut into
    small pieces
1/4 c. margarine, melted
1 c. cheese, shredded

Place fillets in a single layer on a well greased bake and serve platter. Sprinkle with onion, salt and pepper and cover with tomato pieces. Pour margarine over fish and broil until fish flakes easily when tested with a fork. Sprinkle fish with cheese, broil until cheese melts. Makes 4 to 6 servings.

BAKED STUFFED GRAY SEA TROUT
Avis Turcotte

4 slices whole wheat bread, diced
2 tsp. dehydrated onion flakes
2 tbsp. chopped parsley
1/4 tsp. garlic powder
1/4 tsp. poultry seasoning
2 tsp. dehydrated or frozen chives

6 tbsp. chicken bouillon
1 1/2 lbs. sea trout (4 fillets)
    or other fish fillets
Salt and pepper to taste
2 tbsp. oil
Paprika

Combine bread, onion, parsley, garlic powder, poultry seasoning, chives and bouillon. Let stand until liquid is absorbed. Sprinkle cut sides of fillets with salt and pepper. Place 1/2 of fillets, skin side down, in well greased baking dish 12x8x2 inch. Place stuffing on fish, cover with remaining fillets. Brush fish with oil and sprinkle lightly with paprika. Bake at 400° for 20 minutes, basting occasionally, or until fish flakes. Serves 6.

TUNA SWISS PIE
Joan Berry

1 unbaked 9 inch pie shell
1 can (12 1/2 oz.) tuna, drained
    flaked
1 c. shredded swiss cheese
1/2 c. sliced green onion

3 eggs
1 c. mayonnaise
1/2 c. milk

Pierce pastry thoroughly with fork. Bake at 375° for 10 minutes. Remove from oven.

Mix together in large bowl the tuna, cheese and onion. Spoon into pie shell. Stir together remaining ingredients and slowly pour over tuna mixture. Bake at 350° for 50 minutes (or until knife inserted in center comes out clean).

SEAFOOD BEER BATTER　　　　　　　　　　　　　　　　Marie Fagundes

1 1/4 c. self-rising flour　　　　1 egg, beaten
1 tbsp. sugar　　　　　　　　　　 1 c. beer
1 tsp. dry mustard　　　　　　　　Vegetable oil for deep frying
1/4 tsp. cayenne pepper

　　Stir together dry ingredients. Carefully combine egg and beer; slowly stir into flour mixture. Dip seafood into batter and fry a few at a time in hot oil about 3 minutes or until golden brown. Use fish fillets (especially a large Drum) cut into cubes, shrimp, scallops, oysters or clams, all of these are excellent fried with this batter. You may also use this batter to fry onion rings or egg plant cut into french fry size strips.

CAROLINA SUNSET COCKTAIL SAUCE　　　　　　　　　Myrna Peters

1/2 c. chili sauce　　　　　　　 2 tbsp. Lea & Perrins
1/2 c. catsup　　　　　　　　　　2 dash tabasco
4 tbsp. lemon juice　　　　　　　1 tsp. salt
4 tbsp. horseradish

　　Mix all ingredients. Serve with crab or shrimp.

CANDIES, COOKIES

BOURBON BALLS   Marian Hostetter

1 small pkg. vanilla wafers   1 1/2 tbsp. white corn syrup
1 c. chopped nuts   1/3 c. bourbon or rum
1 c. powdered sugar   1 tsp. vanilla
2 tbsp. cocoa

    Roll wafers into fine crumbs. Mix with sugar, cocoa and nuts. Dissolve syrup in bourbon and add to crumb mixture, along with vanilla. Make into small balls and roll in more powdered sugar. Store in coffee can.
    Variation:
    Add 1/3 c. Creme De Menthe instead of bourbon and roll in chocolate sprinkles instead of powdered sugar. Store the same.

CHOCOLATE TOFFEE   Linda Hooper

1/2 c. chopped nuts   1/2 c. butter
3/4 c. packed brown sugar   1 c. semi-sweet chocolate chips

    Sprinkle nuts over bottom of lightly greased 9 inch square pan. Combine sugar and butter in saucepan; bring to rolling boil, stirring constantly. Boil 4-5 minutes to temperature of 270°. Pour over nuts in pan, sprinkle with chocolate chips. Cover for 2 minutes. Spread melted chocolate chips.
    Chill until firm. Remove from pan and break into pieces.
    Servings: 1 pound.

SUGAR PEANUTS   Mrs. Holland

2 c. peanuts (raw-skin on)   1 c. water
1 1/4 c. sugar

    Put in pot together, stir until all water is gone, low fire. Put in large flat pan and put in oven. Bake at 300° for 30-40 minutes.

PEANUT BUTTER BALLS
Pearl O'Neal

1 box 4x sugar
2 sticks butter
1 c. chunky peanut butter
1 tsp. vanilla

    Mix the sugar, butter at room temperature, peanut butter and vanilla together.

Chocolate covering:
6 oz. semi-sweet morsels
1/4 bar wax

    Melt morsels and wax in a double boiler and dip balls in it. Set covered balls on wax paper and let cool.

PEANUT BUTTER FUDGE
Joyce Midgett

1 pkg. (4 serving size) chocolate pudding (NOT INSTANT)
1 c. sugar
1/2 c. milk
1/4 c. peanut butter (creamy or chunky)
1 tbsp. butter

    Combine pudding mix, sugar and milk. Cook until soft ball stage. Remove from heat, add peanut butter and butter. Beat until thick and creamy. Pour into shallow dish. Cut when firm.

PEANUT FUDGE
Joyce Midgett

1 c. sugar
1/2 c. evaporated milk
1 tbsp. margarine
1 c. ground salted peanuts

    Boil sugar and milk, stirring constantly for 5 minutes. Add margarine and peanuts. Mix and spread on buttered plate. Cut while warm.

"REESE" BALLS
Joy Huggett

1 1/2 c. graham cracker crumbs
1 1/3 c. peanut butter
1 box powdered sugar
1 1/2 sticks oleo, melted
12 oz. chocolate chips
2/3 block paraffin

    Combine all but the chocolate chips and paraffin. Roll into walnut size balls. Melt chips and paraffin together and drop balls into mixture. Remove with toothpick and lay on wax paper to cool.

COCONUT PECAN COOKIES   Frances Kapp

1 box yellow cake mix (use dry)   2 eggs
1 box coconut pecan frosting mix   1 stick oleo, melted
   (dry)

Mix well all together and roll into balls the size of a walnut. Place on ungreased cookie sheet and bake at 350° for 10 minutes. Make a chewy cookie.

"COOKIES WHILE YOU SLEEP"

3 egg whites   2/3 c. sugar
1 c. chopped pecans   1 tsp. vanilla
1 c. chocolate chips

Beat egg whites stiff. Gradually add sugar. Fold in nuts, chips and vanilla. Drop by teaspoon onto foil covered cookie sheet. Heat oven to 350°. Place cookies in oven and then turn it off. Leave in oven all night.

NO BAKE COOKIES   Mary Watson

1 lb. sweet chocolate   3 c. corn flakes
1 c. chopped nuts

Melt chocolate over hot water, add nuts and corn flakes. Drop by the spoonful on waxed paper.

CHOCO-CRUMBLE BARS   Norma Phillips

                                        1/2 c. butter, softened
1 1/2 c. all-purpose flour   1 (6 oz.) pkg. semi-sweet choco-
3/4 c. firm-packed brown sugar   late chips
1/4 tsp. salt   1 c. peanut butter

Combine flour, sugar and salt. Cut in butter with pastry blender until mixture resenbles coarse crumbs. Pat mixture into an ungreased 13x9x2 inch baking pan. Bake at 375° for 10 minutes. Cool slightly.

Combine chocolate chips and peanut butter in a small saucepan and cook over low heat until chips melt, stirring constantly. Spread over crust and chill until firm. Cut into bars.

OATMEAL COOKIES
Mrs. Bethany M. Gray

Mix well:
- 2 c. Crisco
- 2 c. granulated sugar
- 2 c. brown sugar
- 1 heaping tsp. cinnamon
- 2 1/2 c. plain flour
- 4 eggs
- 2 tsp. soda
- 1 tsp. salt
- 1 tsp. vanilla
- 1 c. chopped nuts

Stir in:
- 6 c. quick oats

Drop by teaspoon on greased cookie sheets. Bake at 350° for 15-17 minutes. Makes about 10 dozen cookies.

CHEWY OATMEAL COOKIES
Barbara Shimpach

Cream together:
- 3/4 c. shortening, soft
- 1 1/3 c. brown sugar
- 2 eggs
- 1 tsp. vanilla

Sift together:
- 1 c. flour
- 3/4 tsp. soda
- 1 tsp. cinnamon
- 1/4 tsp. nutmeg
- 1/2 tsp. salt

Combine creamed mixture and sifted mixture. Stir in 2 c. Old Fashioned Oatmeal and 1 c. raisins.

Drop by heaping teaspoons on greased cookie sheet. Bake at 350° for 12-15 minutes.

PEANUT BUTTER COOKIES
Laura Scarborough

- 1 c. shortening
- 1 c. granulated sugar
- 1 c. brown sugar
- 1 tsp. vanilla
- 2 eggs
- 1 c. peanut butter
- 2 c. sifted self-rising flour
- 1 c. chopped pecans (if desired)

Cream shortening, sugar, eggs and vanilla. Stir in peanut butter. Sift dry ingredients and stir into creamed mixture. Add pecans. Shape 1 tablespoon of dough. Press into slim "S" shape and place on ungreased cookie sheet. Press dough with back of floured fork to make criss-cross. Bake at 350° for about 10 minutes.

PINEAPPLE COOKIES
                                                    Frances Kapp

1 c. brown sugar, packed   4 c. flour
1 c. granulated sugar   1/4 tsp. salt
1 c. shortening   1 tsp. soda
2 eggs, beaten   1 tsp. vanilla
1 (#2) can crushed pineapple,   1 c. chopped nuts
    drained

Cream shortening and sugars till fluffy; add eggs and rest of ingredients gradually and blend well. Drop by teaspoon on ungreased cookie sheet. Bake at 375° for 12 to 15 minutes. Makes 10 to 12 dozen.

May be frosted with 3/4 c. confectioner's sugar mixed with 2 tbsp. pineapple juice.

PREACHER COOKIES
                                                    Georgia Eason

4 tbsp. cocoa   1/2 c. peanut butter
2 c. sugar   3 c. oatmeal
1/2 c. milk   1 c. of either raisins, coconut
1 stick margarine   or nuts, your choice

Mix in pan, cocoa, sugar, milk and margarine, boil 1 minute. Remove from heat, add peanut butter, oatmeal and your choice of raisins/coconut/nuts. Drop by spoonfuls on wax paper and put in refrigerator until cool. Makes 5 dozen.

SEVEN LAYER COOKIE
                                                    Pearl O'Neal

1 stick butter melted
    Cover with crushed vanilla wafers.
6 oz. semi-sweet morsels
6 oz. butterscotch morsels
Cover with chopped pecans
Cover with coconut
1 can condensed milk

Add ingredients in order in a square baking dish. Bake 30 minutes, or until light brown, at 325°.

SKILLET COOKIES   Linda Hooper

1 lb. pitted dates   1/4 c. butter
1 egg, well beaten   1 c. sugar
2 c. Rice Krispies   1 c. chopped nuts
1 tsp. vanilla   Coconut

In heavy skillet, combine dates, butter, egg and sugar. Cook over low heat until dates are soft (10 minutes) mashing dates with fork while stirring.

Remove from heat, add nuts, Rice Krispies and vanilla. Mix well. Cool, shape into balls and roll in coconut. Servings: 4 dozen.

FRESH APPLE CAKE
Olive Patrick

1 1/2 c. wesson oil	
2 c. sugar	1 tsp. cinnamon
3 eggs	1 tsp. vanilla
3 c. plain flour	3 c. diced apples
1 tsp. salt	1 c. raisins
1 tsp. soda	1 c. chopped nuts (optional)

Cream oil and sugar. Add eggs and vanilla, mix well. Add sifted dry ingredients and beat until blended, batter will be stiff. Add apples, raisins and nuts. Bake at 350° for 1 hour or until done.

APPLE NUT CAKE
Joan Berry

1 1/2 c. sugar   1 c. oil
3 eggs

Mix eggs into sugar, one at a time. Mix well. Add oil and mix thoroughly.

2 c. flour   1 tsp. baking soda
1 tsp. salt   1 tsp. cinnamon

Sift together. Add to oil mixture and beat well. Fold in apples and nuts, and add vanilla:

2 c. sliced apples   1 tsp. vanilla
1/2 c. chopped nuts

Grease and flour an oblong pan. Bake at 350° for about 40 minutes.

APPLESAUCE CAKE
Zenovah Hooper

1/2 c. shortening (1/4 c. butter and 1/4 c. Crisco)	1 tbsp. nutmeg
	1/2 tsp. cloves
2 c. sugar	1 tsp. salt
2 eggs	1 tsp. baking soda
2 c. flour	1 can applesauce
2 tbsp. cinnamon	1 c. pecans
1 tbsp. allspice	

Cream shortening and sugar. Add beaten eggs. Mix dry ingredients, add a little applesauce and dry ingredients to creamed shortening. Add nuts. Bake at 350° for 1 hour.

SAUCY APPLE SWIRL CAKE
Georgia Simons

1/4 c. sugar
2 tsp. cinnamon
1 (17 oz.) pkg. yellow cake mix
1 2/3 c. applecause
3 eggs

Blend sugar and cinnamon. Grease 10 inch Bundt pan and dust with about 1 tbsp. of sugar-cinnamon mixture. Blend cake mix, applesauce and eggs until moist. Beat as directed on package. Reserve 1 1/2 c. batter. Pour remaining batter into pan. Sprinkle with remaining sugar-cinnamon mixture. Top with reserved batter. Bake at $350°$ for 35-45 minutes. Cool cake in pan top side up for 15 minutes. Invert on plate.

CHEESECAKE
Marilyn Davis

1 graham cracker crust
1 (8 oz.) pkg. cream cheese
2 eggs
1/2 c. sugar
3/4 tsp. vanilla

Beat until creamy, do not overbeat. Pour into shell. Bake at $375°$ for 15-20 minutes.

Sour Cream Topping:
1/2 pint sour cream
2-4 tbsp. sugar
1/2 tsp. vanilla

Mix together. Spread carefully on top and bake again for about 5 minutes. Cool, refrigerate.

LEMON CHEESECAKE IN 18 MINUTES
Nina M. Minor

1 (8 oz.) pkg. Borden's cream cheese
2 c. milk
1 pkg. lemon Jello instant pudding
8 inch graham cracker crust

Stir cream cheese until very soft, gradually blend in 1/2 c. milk until smooth and creamy. Add remaining milk and the pudding mix, beat slowly with egg beater (1 minute, do not overbeat). Pour into cooled graham cracker crust, then chill.

CHRISTMAS CAKE   Georgia Eason

2 sticks margarine   2 c. pecans, 1/2 lb.
2 c. sugar   1/2 lb. black walnuts
5 eggs   1 lb. candied cherries
2 c. flour   1 can Baker's coconut
    Mix thoroughly and bake 2 or 2 1/2 hours at 275°. Put a small pan of water in oven while baking.

CREAM OF COCONUT CAKE   Tom Peters

    Bake, according to directions, one box of yellow cake mix in 9x13 inch pan. When done, poke holes all over the top with a meat fork. Let cool and then pour a can of "cream of coconut" over top of cake.
    Then spread 8 oz. container of Cool Whip over it and sprinkle with flaked coconut. Refrigerate.

COCONUT CAKE   Zenovah Hooper

2 c. sifted flour   1 1/3 c. water
1 1/3 c. sugar   4 eggs
3 tsp. baking powder   1/4 c. oil
1 tsp. salt   2 c. coconut
1 pkg. Jello instant vanilla   1 c. nuts
    pudding and pie filling
    Mix all dry ingredients. Add other ingredients. Mix well. Pour into greased and floured pans. Bake at 350° for 35 minutes. Will make three 9 inch layers.

COCONUT CAKE   Mrs. Julian L. Gray

1 pkg. (2 layer size) yellow cake 4 eggs
    mix   1/4 c. oil
1 pkg. (4 serving size) Jello brand 2 c. Baker's Angel Flake
    vanilla instant pudding and   coconut
    pie filling   1 c. chopped walnuts or pecans
1 1/3 c. water   (CONT'D)

Coconut Cake (CONT'D)

    Blend cake mix, pudding mix, water, eggs and oil in large mixer bowl. Beat at medium speed 4 minutes. Stir in coconut and nuts. Pour into three greased and floured 9 inch layer pans. Bake at 350° for 35 minutes. Cool in pans 15 minutes before removing.

FIG CAKE   Sandy Kierzkowski

1/2 c. butter or oleo, softened
1 c. sugar
3 eggs
1/2 tsp. vanilla
2 c. flour
1 tsp. soda
1 tsp. cinnamon
1 tsp. nutmeg
1 c. buttermilk
1 tsp. ground cloves or allspice
1 1/2 c. fig preserves with juice (chopped)
1/2 c. nuts
1/2 c. coconut (optional)
1 c. raisins (optional)

    Cream butter and sugar until light and fluffy. Add eggs one at a time. Stir in vanilla.
    Combine dry ingredients. Add to creamed mixture alternately with buttermilk, mixing well after each addition. Stir in figs, nuts, coconut and raisins.
    Spoon batter into a greased and floured 10 inch tube or bundt pan. Bake at 350° for 50 minutes.

HAWAIIAN CAKE   Ethel O'Neal

1 box Duncan Hines Yellow cake mix
1/2 c. oil
1 small can mandarin oranges (juice and all)
3 eggs, beaten

    Combine cake mix, oil, eggs and juice from oranges. Beat two minutes with electric mixer. Add orange sections and beat until thoroughly chopped and mixed. Bake at 350° in greased and floured pan. Bake in three 9 inch pans for 20 to 25 minutes. Let cool before frosting.   (CONT'D)

Hawaiian Cake (CONT'D)

Frosting:
1 large box Jello vanilla instant pudding
1 (#303) can crushed pineapple and juice
1 (9 oz.) carton Cool Whip

Sprinkle pudding on pineapple and stir in Cool Whip. Put in refrigerator before spreading on cake.

HOT MILK SPONGE CAKE
Zenovah Hooper

4 eggs
2 c. sugar
2 tsp. baking powder
2 c. flour
1/4 tsp. salt
2 tsp. vanilla
2 sticks butter
1 c. milk

Beat eggs first a little. Add sugar. Beat eggs with sugar about 1 minute. Add dry ingredients to this. Heat butter, vanilla and milk until butter melts. Pour over first mixture. Bake in greased layer pans at 350° for 30 minutes. Fill with following:

1/4 c. water
2 squares unsweetened chocolate
4 tbsp. butter
1 c. sugar
1 can Eagle Brand
1 tsp. vanilla

Cook to consistency to spread. Fill cake.

MISSISSIPPI MUD CAKE
Pat Wood and
Priscilla Broadway

2 c. sugar
1 1/2 c. self-rising flour
2 1/2 sticks margarine
1 1/2 c. chopped nuts
1/3 c. cocoa
4 eggs
1 tsp. vanilla
1 1/3 c. coconut
1 (7 oz.) jar marshmallow creme

Cream sugar, cocoa and margarine. Add eggs one at a time; then add vanilla, flour, coconut and nuts. Mix well. Bake at 350° about 30 minutes, in well greased oblong pan.

Remove from oven and spread 1/2 jar of marshmallow creme on cake. Combine 1/2 box 10X sugar, 1 tsp. vanilla, 1/2 stick margarine, 1/4 c. canned milk, 1/4 c. cocoa. Frost cake. Put in refrigerator until cool, cut in squares, and serve.

1-2-3-4 CAKE
Eva Rogerson

1 c. butter
2 c. sugar
3 c. flour
4 eggs (may use 6 for richer cake)

1 tsp. vanilla
1 c. milk

Soften butter at room temperature. Cream butter, add sugar gradually, beating well. Add eggs, one at a time, beating well after each egg. Add milk and flour alternately in three parts. Add vanilla. Bake 15 to 20 minutes or until brown depending on thickness at 350°.

Chocolate Icing:
1/4 c. Crisco
1/3 c. milk
1/2 c. cocoa

1/2 tsp. vanilla
1/4 tsp. salt
3 1/2 c. Confectioner's sugar

Melt Crisco in pan. Add cocoa and salt. Add milk and vanilla mixing well. Add sugar in three parts. Mix until creamy. If too thick add more milk.

PEA-PICKEN CAKE
Norma Phillips

1 box butter cake mix
1 small can mandarin oranges
   (drained)

1/2 c. salad oil
4 eggs

Mix ingredients with mixer. Put in greased and floured 9x13 inch pan. Bake at 350° for 25 minutes. Cool and frost with:

1 large Cool Whip
1 pkg. instant vanilla pudding

1 large can crushed pineapple
   (with syrup)

Mix with spoon and spread on cool cake. Refrigerate.

PINEAPPLE UPSIDE DOWN CAKE
Rita Covey

1/2 stick butter
1/2 c. brown sugar
4 or 5 slices pineapple
1 c. sugar

1 c. self-rising flour
3 eggs
5 tbsp. pineapple juice

Preheat oven to 350°.

Melt butter and brown sugar slowly in a pan. Beat sugar and egg yolks until light. Blend alternately the juice and flour with the beaten yolks and sugar. Beat egg whites until stiff and fold into the above. Place pineapple slices in melted sugar and butter. Pour batter over the pineapple slices. Bake 30 to 40 minutes.

PISTACHIO CAKE
Zenovah Hooper

2 c. sifted flour
1 1/3 c. sugar
3 tsp. baking powder
1 tsp. salt
1 tsp. vanilla
2 pkgs. Royal instant pistachio pudding

1/2 c. Wesson oil
1/2 c. water
1/2 c. milk
4 eggs

Preheat oven to 350°. Grease and flour tube cake pan.
Mix all ingredients except eggs. Add eggs one at a time, beating good between each egg. Beat until smooth.
Bake 1 hour. Cool 15 minutes before removing from pan.

Pistachio Icing:
1 pkg. instant pistachio pudding
1/2 pint whipping cream
1 small Cool Whip

Whip cream until stiff, fold pudding and Cool Whip into whipped cream.

PUMPKIN CAKE
Zenovah Hooper

2 c. sifted flour
1/2 tsp. salt
2 tsp. cinnamon
1/2 tsp. soda
2 tsp. baking powder

Sift all of these ingredients together.

1 c. oil
4 eggs
2 c. pumpkin

Cream these three together. Mix all together. Beat until smooth. Bake at 350° for 30 to 35 minutes. Makes three layers.

Frosting:
8 oz. cream cheese
1 stick margarine
1 tsp. vanilla
1 box confectioner's sugar

SOUR CREAM CAKE
Linda Hooper

2 c. flour (self-rising)
1 3/4 c. sugar
2 eggs
1 tsp. baking powder
1 c. butter
1 tsp. vanilla
1 c. sour cream

Cream butter and sugar. Add sour cream and eggs. Mix thoroughly, add flour and vanilla. (CONT'D)

Sour Cream Cake (CONT'D)

Topping:
3 tbsp. brown sugar   1 1/2 tbsp. butter
1/2 c. walnuts

Cream sugar and butter. Grease and flour pan, put half mixture, spread with half topping, put remaining mixture and spread with rest of topping. Bake at 350° for 45 minutes to 1 hour.

VANILLA WAFER POUND CAKE   Virginia O'Neal

1 1/2 sticks of oleo and 1 1/2 c. sugar, cream together.
1 box (12 oz.) vanilla wafers and 1 (rounded) tsp. baking powder, Crush vanilla wafers and mix in baking powder.
5 eggs, add one at a time to first ingredients and beat 1 tsp. black walnut flavoring. Combine flavoring and first mixture. Add crushed wafers and beat until mixed good.
1 pkg. angel flake cocoanut and 1/2 box raisins, blend these in
   mixture.
   Bake 1 1/2 hours in tube pan at 300° (cook in middle of oven, do not open oven).

WHACKY CAKE   Natalie Swindell

2 c. sugar   1 tsp. salt
3 c. flour   1 tbsp. vinegar
6 tbsp. cocoa   1 tsp. baking soda mixed
1 tsp. vanilla   in 2 c. water
   Mix and bake in 350° oven for 30 to 40 minutes.

WHITE FRUIT CAKE   Georgia Simons

5 eggs   1/2 lb. butter
1 c. white sugar   2 tbsp. vanilla
2 tbsp. lemon extract
   Cream well until light and fluffy.
2 c. all-purpose flour, (reserve small amount to drop fruit in)
   Add to creamed mixture.
2 c. chopped pecans   1 lb. candied pineapple
3/4 lb. candied cherries
   Mix into the reserved flour and stir into batter.   (CONT'D)

White Fruit Cake (CONT'D)

Pour into large tube pan that has been greased and floured. Bake at 325° for 1 hour and 20 minutes.
Turn out after cooling for 10 minutes. Glaze with 2 tbsp. white corn syrup that has been heated hot.

COCONUT CAKE FILLING
Zenovah Hooper

1 egg yolk
1 c. milk
1 c. sugar
1 tbsp. cornstarch
1 tsp. vanilla
1 grated coconut

Mix together all ingredients except coconut. Cook in double boiler over low heat until thickened. Cool partly, then add coconut before icing cake.

COCONUT AND PECAN FROSTING
Mrs. Julian L. Gray

Combine:
1 c. evaporated milk
1 c. sugar
3 eggs, beaten
1/2 c. butter or margarine
1 tsp. vanilla

Cook and stir over medium heat until thickened, about 12 minutes.
Add:
1 1/3 c. Baker's angel flake coconut
1 c. chopped pecans

Beat until thick enough to spread between layers, frost top and sides of cake.

COCONUT CREAM CHEESE FROSTING
Zenovah Hooper

4 tbsp. margarine
2 c. coconut
1 pkg. (8 oz.) cream cheese
2 tsp. milk
3 1/2 c. confectioner's sugar
1 tsp. vanilla

Melt 2 tbsp. margarine in skillet. Add coconut. Stir constantly over low heat until golden brown. Spread coconut on absorbent paper to cool.
(CONT'D)

Coconut Cream Cheese Frosting (CONT'D)

Cream 2 tbsp. butter with cream cheese, add milk. Beat in sugar gradually. Blend in vanilla. Stir in 1 3/4 c. of coconut. Spread on tops of cake layers. Stack and sprinkle with remaining coconut.

CREAM CHEESE FROSTING
Laura Scarborough

1 (1 lb.) pack confectioner's sugar
2 (3 oz.) pkgs. cream cheese, softened
1/3 c. butter
1 tsp. milk
1 1/2 tsp. vanilla
1/2 tsp. cream of tartar

Combine all ingredients and beat until frosting is creamy and smooth. If desired, replace butter with additional cream cheese.

AUTUMN APPLE PIE

6 medium apples, cored, peeled and sliced
1 c. flour
1/2 c. sugar
1 tbsp. cinnamon
1/2 c. margarine

Arrange apple slices in a greased 8 inch square baking dish. Bake on top rack in preheated 425° oven for 15 minutes.

Meanwhile, in bowl mix well flour, sugar, and cinnamon. With fork work in margarine until crumbly. Sprinkle over apples. Bake 10 to 15 minutes until topping is lightly browned.

Makes 8 servings. Can be topped with milk, cream or ice cream.

BUTTERSCOTCH PIE   Lucretia Midgett

1 c. brown sugar
2 tbsp. water
1 c. cold water
5 tbsp. flour
2 egg yolks
1 c. evaporated milk
1/2 tsp. vanilla

Boil sugar with two tablespoons water to a thick syrup (about 5 minutes). Make a smooth paste of cold water and flour. Add to syrup and boil one minute, stirring constantly. Beat egg yolks, add milk and combine with sugar mixture. Cook over boiling water 10 minutes or until thick enough to drop in sheets from side of spoon. Add vanilla, mix well. Pour into baked pie shell. Cover with meringue and brown in a slow oven.

CHERRY CREAM CHEESE PIE   Zenovah Hooper

1 (9 inch) graham cracker pie shell
1 pkg. (8 oz.) cream cheese
1 1/3 c. (15 oz.) sweetened condensed milk
1/3 c. fresh or bottled lemon juice
1 tsp. vanilla
1 can prepared cherry pie filling

Soften cream cheese. Whip until fluffy. Add milk, continue to beat until blended. Add lemon juice and vanilla, blend well. Pour into prepared graham cracker crust. Chill 2 to 3 hours.

Garnish top of pie with cherry pie filling.

CHOCOLATE CHESS PIE
Peggy Weinfurtner

1 3/4 c. sugar
1/3 c. cocoa
1 1/4 c. butter, melted
2 (9 inch) unbaked pie shells

4 eggs, beaten
1/4 c. evaporated milk
1 tsp. vanilla

Combine sugar, cocoa and butter. Add eggs, milk and vanilla, mixing thoroughly. Pour into pie shells. Serve with whipped cream or ice cream. Bake at 350° for 35 to 40 minutes.

EXQUISITE PIE
Nina M. Minor

1 stick margarine, melted
1 c. sugar
2 eggs, beaten
1 tbsp. vinegar

1/2 c. raisins (floured)
1 tsp. vanilla
1/2 c. chopped nuts
1/2 c. coconut

Mix all ingredients in order listed. Pour into uncooked pie crust, bake for 30 minutes in 350° oven.

GERMAN SWEET CHOCOLATE CREAM PIE
Zenovah Hooper

1 pkg. (4 oz.) Baker's German
    Sweet chocolate
1/3 c. milk
2 tbsp. sugar
1 pkg. (3 oz.) cream cheese

1 (8 oz.) Cool Whip
1 pkg. graham cracker crust

Heat chocolate and 2 tbsp. milk over low heat, stirring until melted. Beat sugar into cream cheese; add remaining milk and chocolate mixture, beat until smooth. Fold Cool Whip into chocolate mixture and blend until smooth. Spoon mixture into crust. Freeze about 4 hours.'

COCONUT PIE
Zenovah Hooper

1/2 c. sugar
1/4 c. flour
1 1/2 c. milk, scalded
3 eggs, separated

2 tbsp. butter
1 tsp. vanilla
Few drops of nutmeg and
    cinnamon

(CONT'D)

Coconut Pie (CONT'D)

    Combine sugar and flour. Add scalded milk. Cook over direct heat until thick. Beat eggs, real good, add a little of hot mixture. Add eggs, cook in double boiler 2 minutes.
    Add vanilla, butter, nutmeg and cinnamon and cool.
    Beat egg whites until stiff, adding 6 tbsp. sugar. Add one-third of egg whites and coconut. Pour in baked pastry shell. Brown at 450° with remainder of egg whites for topping.

CRANBERRY-WALNUT PIE   Joy Huggett

1 1/2 c. corn syrup   1 c. chopped cranberries
1/2 c. sugar   1 c. chopped walnuts
4 eggs   1 tbsp. grated orange rind
2 tbsp. melted oleo   1 unbaked pie shell
    Beat corn syrup, sugar, eggs and oleo together. Add cranberries, walnuts and orange rind. Pour into unbaked pie shell and bake at 350° for one hour or until set. Chill.

LEMON MERINGUE PIE   Mrs. Asa Gray, Jr.

1 can Eagle Brand milk   2 eggs
2 lemons   1 dash salt
    Separate egg yolks from whites; beat yolks well. Mix milk and egg yolks, add juice from lemons. Put in dash of salt.
    Line pie pan with finely crumbled vanilla wafers and do sides with whole wafers. Pie pan may be greased with butter or shortening. Pour mixture in pie crust. Top with white of eggs beaten stiff. Bake in oven until frosting is lightly brown.

PEACHY PRALINE PIE   Georgia Simons

3/4 c. granulated sugar   3 tbsp. flour
    Combine in a large bowl. Add:
4 c. sliced peeled peaches   1 1/2 tsp. lemon juice
    Combine in small bowl until mixture is crumbly.
1/3 c. brown sugar, firmly packed   1/4 c. flour
1/2 c. chopped pecans   3 tbsp. butter, melted
                                                        (CONT'D)
1 unbaked pie shell

Peachy Praline Pie (CONT'D)

Sprinkle one third of pecan mixture over bottom of pie shell; cover with the peach mixture and sprinkle remaining pecan mixture over peaches. Bake in hot oven (400°) until peaches are tender, about 40 minutes.

PEANUT PIE
Mary M. Watson

1/2 c. margarine
1 c. sugar
3 eggs
3 tsp. vinegar
1 tsp. vanilla
1/2 c. chopped toasted peanuts
Unbaked pie shell

Toast raw blanched peanuts. Melt margarine, add ingredients in order listed. Mix thoroughly. Pour into pie shell, bake 30 minutes at 350°.

PECAN PIE
Marilyn Davis

3 eggs
2/3 c. sugar
1 c. dark corn syrup
1/3 c. melted butter or margarine
1 c. pecan halves
1 (9 inch) unbaked pastry shell

Beat eggs thoroughly with sugar, dash of salt, corn syrup and melted butter. Add pecans. Pour into shell. Bake at 350° for 50 minutes. Cool.

PUMPKIN PIE
Wilma Midgett

1 1/2 c. canned pumpkin
2/3 c. brown sugar
1 tsp. cinnamon
1/2 tsp. ginger
2 eggs
1 c. milk
1 c. cream

Line a 9 inch pie pan with pastry, making a high edge. Brush pastry all over with egg white. Place in refrigerator while preparing filling. Mix pumpkin and the spices. Sift brown sugar onto pumpkin and mix well. Beat eggs and add, then add milk and cream and mix well. Place crust in oven and carefully pour filling in. Bake at 450° for 10 minutes then reduce to 350° and bake 45 minutes more until the custard is set.

CUSTARD PIE CRUST
Ruth Foley

2 c. flour
1 tsp. salt
1/2 tbsp. sugar
1/4 c. cold water

1 egg, beaten
1/2 tbsp. vinegar
1 c. shortening

Cut shortening into flour, salt and sugar (mixed). Add water, egg and vinegar. Fill with favorite custard recipe. (Does not get "soggy"!)

APPLE DUMPLINS' IN MILK
Lennie Midgett

1 can evaporated milk
1 1/2 cans water
2 1/2 c. sugar

2 tsp. vanilla
4 large apples, peel and slice

In a large covered saucepan mix milk, water and sugar and cook until sugar dissolves. Add flavoring. Place dumplins' in milk mixture and boil until done, turning each one once (about 1/2 hour).

Dumplins':
3 c. flour (self-rising)
1 tsp. salt

1 1/4 c. shortening
Enough water to make soft dough

Mix and divide dough into 10 parts. Roll out and put sliced apples in center and fold dough over into ball. Cook as above.

APPLE JACK'S
Arretta Midgett

Filling:
6 large apples, peeled and sliced
1/4 c. water

1/2 c. sugar
1/2 tsp. cinnamon

Mix and cook slowly over low heat until apples are tender.

Crust:
2 c. flour
1 tsp. salt
1 tsp. baking powder

3/4 c. shortening
1/3 c. cold water

Sift together flour, salt and baking powder. Cut in shortening. Blend water into mixture a little at a time. Chill for about 15 minutes. Roll out chilled dough into 8 or 10 small circles 1/8 inch thick. Spoon 2 heaping tbsp. of filling into center of each circle, and fold. Press edges together with floured fork. Fry on low flame in 2 tbsp. of oil (or just enough to keep from sticking) until golden on each side.

BAKED APPLES
                                    Mrs. Bethany M. Gray

Take 10 or 12 big, juicy apples.
Peel and core. Butter a baking dish, and put in apples. Fill center with sugar. Take 1/2 teacup of butter and 1 tbsp. flour, rub together until smooth. To this, put enough boiling water to cover each apple. Sprinkle nutmeg over apples. Bake in slow oven 1 hour or longer. Can be eaten with meat or used as a dessert.

APPLE OATMEAL CRISP
                                    Avis Turcotte

2 lbs. cooking apples   2 tbsp. orange juice
1/4 c. dark brown sugar   1/2 c. flour
1/2 tsp. cinnamon   1/2 c. oatmeal
1/2 tsp. nutmeg   1/4 tsp. salt
1 tbsp. lemon juice   6 tbsp. oleo
Grated rind of 1 orange

Peel, core and slice apples. Sprinkle 1/4 c. sugar over apples. Add cinnamon and nutmeg, toss, sprinkle on lemon juice, orange rind and orange juice, toss. Pack into deep pie plate, press lightly on top. Mix flour, oatmeal and salt. Cut in the oleo. Sprinkle over apples and press firmly. Bake at 375° for 45 minutes. Serve warm.

BLITZENTORTE
                                    Jackie Pfost

Cream 1/2 c. butter and 1/2 c. sugar together. Add 4 egg yolks, BEAT. Sift together, 1 c. flour and 1 tsp. baking powder. Add alternately with 4 tbsp. milk, add 1 tsp. vanilla. Mix very well. Spread in two layers (thin) Bake 15 minutes at 375°.
Beat egg whites VERY stiff with 1 c. sugar. Spread on baked layers and sprinkle with lots of walnuts (1 c.) lightly brown in hot oven. Cool about 10 minutes, remove from pans topside down on plate, fill with whipped cream; add second layer topside UP. *be sure cake is cool before adding whip cream.

FRESH BLUEBERRY COBBLER
Gem Minor

6 c. blueberries
1/2 to 3/4 c. sugar
    (depending on tartness of berries)
4 tbsp. flour
1 tsp. ground cinnamon
1 tbsp. butter
1/2 recipe pie pastry (rolled out)

Wash berries, drain. Mix sugar, flour and cinnamon together. Fold into berries, pour into greased casserole or utility dish. Dot with butter. Cover with pastry, prick with fork. Bake at 400° for 25 to 30 minutes or until golden brown. Serve warm.

BLUEBERRY PUDDING
Karen Austin

1 stick of margarine
2 c. sugar
1 1/2 c. self-rising flour
1 1/2 c. milk
2 c. blueberries

Melt margarine in a 2 quart casserole. Mix sugar, flour and milk. Add fruit after you pour mix into butter. DO NOT STIR AFTER THE FRUIT IS ADDED IN A HEAP IN THE CENTER OF THE CASSEROLE. Bake at 350° for 30 to 45 minutes.

BREAD PUDDING
Pearl Covey

Beat 4 eggs with fork well. Add:
1 c. sugar
2 cans water
2 (4 oz.) cans evaporated milk
2 tsp. vanilla

Mix the above well. Tear dried bread and mix well into above until almost all of the liquid is absorbed. Put into 9x13 inch pan and sprinkle top well with nutmeg. Bake at 250° approximately 1 hour or until knife comes out clean.

CHERRY DESSERT
Pearl Covey

Graham Cracker Crust:
1/3 c. butter, (softened)
2 tbsp. sugar
10 graham crackers, whole, then crush into crumbs

Work together the above. Chill in pan right away. (CONT'D)

Cherry Dessert (CONT'D)

1 pkg. of Dream Whip, made
    Add:
15 oz. can of Eagle Brand milk   1 tsp. vanilla
1/3 c. lemon juice
    Pour on chilled crust.
    Add 1 can cherry pie filling to top with 2 tbsp. sugar. Chill.

EASY COBBLER   Joy Huggett

1 can apple pie filling   1 1/2 c. sugar
1 can peaches (cube, don't drain)   1 stick oleo
1 1/2 c. Bisquick
    Layer pie filling and peaches in a 9x13 inch pan. Mix Bisquick and sugar and spread over fruit. Cut oleo into pieces and dot over Bisquick. Bake at 350° for 40 to 50 minutes. Good with ice cream.

CRANBERRY DESSERT   Pearl Covey

    Grind 1 pkg. cranberries and add 1 1/2 c. sugar. Let stand 2 hours. Add:
1 (#2) can crushed pineapple which   1/2 c. sugar
    has been drained   1 pkg. Dream Whip, prepared
1 lb. pkg. miniature marshmallows
3/4 c. chopped nuts
    Put in container and refrigerate. This will keep several days.

PEACH-APPLE CRISP   Marilyn Davis

2 c. sliced peaches/apples   1/2 tsp. cinnamon
1/3 to 1/2 c. brown sugar   1/2 tsp. nutmeg
1/4 c. flour   3 tbsp. soft butter
1/4 c. oats
    Place peaches/apples in greased loaf pan 9x5x3 inch. Blend remaining ingredients until crumbly. Spread over top. Bake at 350° for 30 minutes. Serve warm.

PINEAPPLE SURPRISE
Joyce Midgett

3 eggs, well beaten
2 c. sugar
1 (20 oz.) can pineapple, crushed and undrained
4 c. fresh bread cubes
1/2 c. margarine (cut into small pieces)
1/2 to 1 c. raisins (optional)

Combine all ingredients, mix well. Pour into greased baking pan. Bake at 350° for 1 hour. Let cool. Cut into 12 squares.

WILLA PFAU'S DESSERT
Georgia Simons

Melt 1 stick of butter in a 9x13 inch pan. Mix in pan 1 c. of flour and 1/2 c. nuts. Press down in bottom of pan. Bake at 350° for 15 minutes. Cool.

Cream until fluffy 1 pkg. (large) cream cheese and 1 c. brown sugar. Add 1/2 carton of large Cool Whip by folding in. Spread this mixture over cooled crust in pan. Beat until thick 3 c. milk and 2 large pkgs. of vanilla instant pudding. Put this mixture on the cream cheese mixture. Top with rest of Cool Whip and add crushed nuts on top.

CARDINAL STRAWBERRIES
Marilyn Davis

1 quart fresh strawberries
1/4 c. raspberry jam
2 tbsp. sugar
1/4 c. water
1 tbsp. Kirsch (cherry liquor)
1/4 c. slivered almonds

Wash and hull strawberries. Combine jam, sugar and water in saucepan, and simmer about 2 minutes. Add the Kirsch and chill.

Arrange strawberries in four dishes. Pour the chilled sauce over the fruit and sprinkle with the slivered almonds.

Serve with plain cookies (such as sugar or butter cookies).

CHOCOLATE ICE CREAM TOPPING
Barbara Shimpach

Combine in saucepan:
2 squares unsweetened chocolate
1 c. sugar
1 c. light corn syrup
1/2 c. evaporated milk
1/4 tsp. salt
3 tbsp. oleo

Cook over medium heat, stirring constantly until mixture comes to a full rolling boil. Boil 3 minutes, stirring occasionally. Remove from heat.

(CONT'D)

Chocolate Ice Cream Topping (CONT'D)

　　Stir in 1 tsp. vanilla. Cool slightly then beat for about 1 minute with rotary beater. Serve warm over vanilla ice cream.

SWEETENED CONDENSED MILK   Zoe Northington

1 c. instant non-fat dry milk　　　1/3 c. boiling water
2/3 c. sugar　　　　　　　　　　　3 tbsp. butter or oleo
　　Melt butter in boiling water. Blend with sugar and milk in blender or beat well. Can be stored in refrigerator or used at once in any recipe calling for Eagle Brand or others.

BAKED BEANS   Janice Moher

2 cans pork and beans   2 tbsp. catsup
2 tbsp. molasses   1 diced onion
2 tbsp. mustard   1 tbsp. bacon grease
    Mix all together and bake for 30 minutes at 350°.

GREEN BEAN CASSEROLE   Ann Frivett

1 can French style green beans   1 can french fried onions
1 can cream of mushroom soup
    Drain green beans, combine with soup and 1/2 can onions. Pour into greased 1 quart casserole. Bake at 350° for 20 minutes. Garnish with remaining onions and bake 5 minutes longer.

BROCCOLI CASSEROLE   Mrs. C.G. Webber

1 c. cooked rice   1 small can evaporated milk
2 pkgs. cooked broccoli   Dash garlic salt
3/4 of an 8 oz. jar Cheese Whiz 1 c. buttered bread crumbs
1 can cream of celery soup   Dash paprika
    Heat cheese, soup, milk...mix with broccoli and rice. Top with buttered crumbs/paprika. Bake in casserole at 350° for 20-30 minutes.

CARROTS SUPREME

    Cook 8 large carrots; washed, scraped and cut into 1 inch rounds. Drain.
    Mix the following and stir into cooked carrots:
1/2 c. cherry preserves   1 tsp. spicy mustard
1/4 c. apricot preserves   1 tbsp. sherry or lemon juice
1/4 c. pineapple preserves   Salt, if needed
    Reheat carrots for a few minutes.

BAKED CORN
Georgia Simons

1/4 c. butter
1/2 tsp. salt
1/4 c. flour
3 egg whites, beaten stiff
2/3 c. milk
3 egg yolks, beaten
1 (#303) can cream corn

    Melt butter, add flour and blend. Add milk and corn. Cook until thick. Remove from fire. Add egg yolks and salt. Fold in whites. Bake in greased 2 quart baking dish 45 minutes at $325°$.

CREAM PEAS
Rita Covey

1 can peas
2 tbsp. oleo
1 tbsp. sugar
Salt to taste
2 tbsp. flour
1/4 c. milk

    In saucepan, mix peas, oleo, sugar, salt and flour well before turning on heat. Cook over low heat until thick, then add milk. I use evaporated milk undiluted. You may use fresh milk. If too thick for your taste add more milk to thin.

GOLDEN POTATO CASSEROLE
Alys Conley

6 medium potatoes
1/4 c. butter
2 c. sour cream
2 c. shredded cheddar cheese
1/3 c. onion, chopped
1 tsp. salt and 1 tsp. pepper

    Cook potatoes in skin. Chill. Peel and grate in large bowl. In medium pan over low heat, combine butter and cheese. Stir occasionally until cheese melts. Remove from heat and blend in sour cream and onions. Lightly blend this into the grated potatoes. Place in buttered 2 quart casserole and dot with butter (2 tbsp.) Bake at $325°$ to $350°$ for 45 minutes.

RUTABAGA ONION CASSEROLE
Joyce Midgett

3 c. thinly sliced onion
2 rutabagas, sliced
Salt and pepper to taste
1 chicken bouillon cube
1/2 c. boiling water
2 tbsp. butter

    Arrange alternate layers of rutabaga and onions in a greased 2 quart casserole. Sprinkle layers with salt and pepper. Dissolve bouillon in boiling water and pour over vegetables. Dot with butter. Cover and bake at $400°$ for 1 1/4 hours or until rutabagas are tender. 6 servings.

SQUASH CASSEROLE
Kiki Caldwell

Cook 3 or 4 large Summer squash in a large pan for about 15 minutes. Drain and add 1/2 c. margarine, salt and pepper. Let cool.

When cool, place 1/2 of squash in a casserole. Top with 5 slices American cheese and then 1 c. of bread crumbs.

Place remaining squash in casserole and top that with 5 more slices of cheese and another cup of bread crumbs.

Bake at 350° for 20 to 25 minutes or till bubbling.

SWEET POTATO BALLS
Marie Fagundes

3 c. cooked yams or sweet potatoes, mashed and run through strainer
1/4 c. butter
3/4 c. brown sugar
2 tbsp. milk
1/4 tsp. salt
1/2 tsp. grated lemon rind
8 large marshmallows
1/2 c. crushed corn flakes

In mixing bowl, combine potatoes, butter, sugar, milk, salt and lemon rind. With a tablespoon scoop up about 1/4 c. of mixture, place a marshmallow in the center, cover with more potato mixture, shape in balls. Roll each ball in crushed corn flakes. Place in buttered baking dish and bake at 375° until marshmallows begin to ooze, about 20 minutes. Makes 8 balls.

SWEET POTATO CASSEROLE
Mrs. Bethany M. Gray

3 c. cooked sweet potatoes
1/2 c. sugar
1/2 tsp. salt
1/2 c. evaporated milk
2 eggs, beaten
1 stick margarine, melted
1/2 tsp. vanilla

Mix well together and put in baking dish.

Topping:
1/2 c. brown sugar
1/3 c. all-purpose flour
1 stick margarine, melted
1 c. nuts, broken

Mix together and spread over the sweet potato mixture. Bake at 350° for 35 minutes.

VEGETABLE CASSEROLE
Joy Huggett

Steam until tender:
1 c. chopped onion and 1 c. chopped celery
   Add:
2 pkgs. frozen mixed vegetables, cooked
   Mix:
3/4 c. mayonnaise   2 tbsp. soft butter
1 c. grated cheddar cheese

Mix this with the above vegetables, onion and celery. Place in casserole and top with <u>Ritz Crackers</u>. Dot with 2 tbsp. butter and bake at 375° for 30 to 35 minutes.

IMPOSSIBLE VEGETABLE PIE
Virginia O'Neal

2 c. chopped fresh broccoli   1 1/2 c. milk
   or sliced fresh cauliflower   3/4 c. Bisquick baking mix
1/2 c. chopped onion   3 eggs
1/2 c. chopped green pepper   1 tsp. salt
1 c. shredded cheddar cheese   1/4 tsp. pepper

Heat oven to 400°. Lightly grease 10 inch pie plate. Bring 1 c. of water to a boil, add 1/2 tsp. salt, add broccoli, cover and cook until almost tender, about 5 minutes. Drain. Mix broccoli, onion, green pepper and cheese in pie plate. Beat remaining ingredients until smooth, pour into pie plate. Bake until golden brown and knife inserted halfway between center and edge comes out clean, 35 to 40 minutes. Let stand 5 minutes before serving.

*1 pkg. frozen chopped broccoli or cauliflower, thawed and drained can be substituted for the fresh. Do not cook.

ZUCCHINI
Alys Conley

Butter a 9x13 inch pan
Slice zucchini into 1/2 inch rounds and place in pan.
Top each round with:
A slice of tomato
A thin slice of onion
A ring of pepper
Crumbled Crisp Bacon
Parmesan cheese
   Bake at 350° for 1 hour.

ZUCCHINI PIE
Patricia Midgett

2 onions
5-6 medium zucchini
7 medium or 6 large eggs, beaten
1/4 c. oil
1 1/2 c. salted cracker crumbs
1/2 lb. mozzarella cheese, grated
1/2 c. parmesan cheese, grated
Salt, pepper and garlic powder to taste

Mix all together. Pour evenly into 2 (9 inch) pie pans. Sprinkle top with parsley and paprika. Bake in 350° oven for 30 to 35 minutes. Eat one and freeze one.

ITALIAN DELIGHT
Trisha Sandelli

1 lb. spaghetti
1 stick butter
Garlic salt

Cook spaghetti according to package. Melt butter in hot spaghetti, after draining. Add garlic salt to taste. Serve hot or cold.

ANGIES MEXICAN RICE
Avis Turcotte

1 c. rice
Oil
1 chopped onion
1 (6 oz.) can tomato sauce
1 c. hot water or chicken broth

Fry rice in heated oil and stir until browned. Add onion and tomato sauce and liquid. Cover and cook until liquid is absorbed.

WILD RICE
Marilyn Davis

Prepare package of Uncle Ben's Wild and Long-Grained rice. Add:
Mushrooms and onions browned in skillet with chicken bits
2 tbsp. wine
1 chicken bouillon cube

Sprinkle with bacon bits.

ZUCCHINI CASSEROLE — Lee Warren

3 c. squash
2 carrots, grated
1 small onion, grated
1/2 c. sour cream

1 c. undiluted cream of chicken soup
1/2 bag Pepperidge Farm Dressing
1/3 c. melted butter

Cut sqash bite size. Boil 10 minutes or until done, drain. Add carrots and onion, sour cream and chicken soup. Mix 1/2 bag Pepperidge Farm Dressing with butter. Add 1/2 to the above and mix well. Pour into greased casserole dish. Top with remaining dressing. Bake at 325° for 45 minutes.

SALADS AND
MISCELLANEOUS

THREE BEAN SALAD
Virginia O'Neal

1 can (16 oz.) French Cut Green Beans
1 can (16 oz.) Yellow Wax Beans
1 can (16 oz.) Red Kidney Beans
1 can (16 oz.) Bean Sprouts
1/2 c. Green peppers, minced
1/2 c. green onion tops, chopped
1/2 c. cider vinegar
1/3 c. salad oil
3/4 c. sugar
Salt and pepper to taste
1 rib of celery, chopped (optional)

Mix together, let stand in refrigerator overnight. Serves 10.

THREE BEAN SALAD
Beverly Nobel

1 c. kidney beans
1 c. each green and wax beans
4 small onions, sliced and separate the rings
3/4 c. wine vinegar
1 c. sugar

Mix the above with between 1/2 and 1/3 c. salad oil.

CAULIFLOWER SALAD
Evelyn McComas

Medium head of cauliflower, sliced
1 pkg. frozen peas, cooked and drained
1 small onion, chopped
3 stalks celery, sliced
1 c. mayonnaise mixed with 4 tbsp. milk and 1/2 tsp. salt and pepper

Mix and marinate overnight in a tight container in the refrigerator.
(1 c. of cheddar cheese cubes may be added before serving).

CHERRY JELLO SALAD
Marie Fagundes

1 pkg. cherry jello
1 (#303) can pitted dark sweet cherries, drained, reserve juice
1 small pkg. Philadelphia cream cheese, cut into small pieces
1 c. miniature marshmallows

Mix jello, cream cheese, and marshmallows; add 1 c. boiling water. Using a fork, stir and mash pieces of cream cheese until they are of pea size pieces. Take reserved cherry juice and add enough cold water to make a cup; stir into the jello mixture. Pour
(CONT'D)

Cherry Jello Salad (CONT'D)

into desired jello mold or dish, place in refrigerator. When jello is almost set, stir in cherries, return to refrigerator. One half cup chopped pecans or English walnuts may be added if desired at the same time you stir in the cherries.

FINGER JELLO   Marilyn Davis

4 pkgs. unflavored gelatin   1/2 c. sugar
1 c. cold water   4 c. boiling water
3 small packs Jello
    Mix all of the above and pour into 4 sided cookie sheet. Let set overnight in refrigerator. (Can also use lasagna pans).
    Cut into designs with cookie cutters. Transport in plastic bags if necessary.

LUCRETIA'S FRUIT SALAD   Lucretia Midgett

1 lb., 4 oz. can pineapple chunks   1 c. miniature marshmallows
2 cans mandarin oranges   1/3 c. mayonnaise
1/3 c. chopped pecans
    Drain pineapple chunks and mandarin oranges. Mix pineapple, oranges, pecans and marshmallows. Add mayonnaise, toss lightly and refrigerate. Serve in salad bowl lined with lettuce leaves. Makes 6 to 8 servings.

FRUIT SALAD   Kiki Caldwell

1 can pineapple chunks (do not   2 sliced bananas
    drain)   3 apples, chopped
1 can sliced pears (<u>drained</u>)   1 c. hopped nuts
1 can mandarin oranges (do not   1 can peach pie filling
    drain)
    Mix and chill.

JELLO SALAD
Zenovah Hooper

1 can (14 1/2 oz.) crushed pineapple
1 carton (12 oz.) Lite and Lively
  cottage cheese
1 Cool Whip (9 oz.)
1 pkg. strawberry jello

Heat pineapple to boiling. Remove from heat and add dry Jello. Let cool. Blend mixture with cottage cheese and Cool Whip. Chill.

SPICED PEACH GELATIN SALAD
Emily Landrum

Peach syrup
1/4 c. white vinegar
1/2 c. sugar
12 whole cloves
2 sticks cinnamon
Hot water
6 oz. pkg. orange gelatin
1 large can sliced peaches,
  drained

Drain peaches. Combine syrup, vinegar, sugar and spices. Simmer 15 minutes over low heat. Strain mixture and add enough hot water to make two cups. Dissolve gelatin in hot liquid and chill until slightly thickened. Fold in peaches and place in wet one quart mold. Chill until firm. Unmold on a platter lined with salad greens.

LAYERED VEGETABLE SALAD
Marguerite Altemus

Layer in 9x13 inch glass or plastic pan:
1 head of lettuce, torn, not cut
1 large Bermuda onion, sliced thin
1 large head cauliflower, raw,
  sliced
1 (10 oz.) pkg. frozen peas, thawed,
  uncooked
1 lb. bacon, chopped, fried crisp,
  drained
4 hard boiled eggs, sliced; salt and pepper
1/2 c. green pepper, diced
1/2 c. parmesan cheese, grated
2 c. mayonnaise mixed with
  1/2 c. sugar
Top with grated sharp cheese

Refrigerate overnight.

QUICK AND EASY SAUSAGE SALAD
Sarah Midgett

1/2 pkg. (3-4 oz.) elbow macaroni
1 c. sour cream
1/4 c. sweet pickle relish
    (drained)
1/4 c. chopped green peppers
1/4 c. chopped onion
3 tbsp. vinegar
2 c. cubed cheddar cheese
1 lb. salami, cut in 1/2 inch cubes

    Cook macaroni according to package directions, drain well. In large bowl, toss macaroni with sour cream, pickle relish, green pepper, onion, vinegar and mustard. Fold in cheese and salami. Chill to blend flavors. Makes 6 cups.

SPINACH-ORANGE SALAD
Mrs. C.G. Webber

1 (10 oz.) bag fresh spinach
12 medium mushrooms, sliced thin
1 small onion, diced
1 (16 oz.) can mandarin oranges, drained

    Rinse and stem spinach. Dry it well and tear into bite-sized pieces. Tos with Honey Dressing.

Honey Dressing:
1 c. mayonnaise
3 tbsp. honey
1 tbsp. lemon juice

    Combine mayonnaise with honey and lemon juice. Beat with a small wire whisk until smooth/good consistency. Serves 8.
    (Cucumbers or avocado can be added).

WATERGATE SALAD
Zenovah Hooper

1 pkg. Pistachio instant pudding and pie filling
1 Cool Whip (9 oz.)
1 can crushed pineapple with juice
1 c. miniature marshmallows
1/2 c. chopped pecans

    Mix all ingredients together. Chill one hour.

WATERGATE SALAD
Anna Pendleton

1 pkg. instant Pistachio pudding
1 (15 oz.) can crushed pineapple
1/2 c. miniature marshmallows
1/2 c. chopped nuts
1 c. Cool Whip

    Put pudding mixture in a bowl, add pineapple with juice and stir, add marshmallows and nuts, mix together, stir in Cool Whip. Chill prior to serving.

FRENCH DRESSING   Mrs. C.G. Webber

1/4 c. vinegar   1 tsp. salt
1 c. salad oil   1 tsp. mustard (dry)
1/2 c. sugar   1 tsp. paprika

Put all ingredients in blender and mix until well blended and sugar is dissolved. Pour in a bottle with a screw top. Shake well each time before using.

CREAMY HERBAL DRESSING   J.L. Seagull Restaurant

Small: Large:
1 c. mayonnaise   4 c. mayonnaise
1/2 tbsp. lemon juice   2 tbsp. lemon juice
1/4 tsp. salt   1 tsp. salt
1/4 tsp. paprika   1 tsp. paprika
1/2 tsp. thyme   2 tsp. thyme
1/2 tsp. marjoram   2 tsp. marjoram
1/2 tsp. parsley   2 tsp. parsley
1/2 tsp. oregano   2 tsp. oregano
1 tbsp. grated onion   4 tbsp. grated onion
1 clove grated garlic   4 cloves grated garlic
1/8 tsp. curry powder   1/2 tsp. curry powder
1 c. sour cream   4 c. sour cream

Thin with whole milk.

SALAD DRESSING   Zenovah Hooper

1 can Borden's sweetened   1 tsp. mustard
    condensed milk   1 tsp. salt
2 eggs
1 c. vinegar

Beat eggs. Add mustard mixed in a little water. Stir in vinegar slowly and then milk. Store in jars.

CHEESE BALL
Laura Scarborough

2 lbs. cream cheese (softened at room temperature)
1/4 c. chopped green pepper
2 tsp. grated onion
2 tsp. seasoned salt
8 oz. can drained crushed pineapple
2 c. chopped pecans (reserve 1 c. nuts to roll cheese ball in).

Mix together, then roll in nuts.

HOT MEXICAN DIP
Marilyn Davis

1 small can chopped green chiles
1 small can chopped black olives
2 large tomatoes (chopped fine)
6 to 8 green onions with tops (chopped)
3 tbsp. olive oil
1 1/2 tbsp. wine vinegar
1/2 tsp. garlic salt

Mix and chill 2 to 4 hours. Drain before serving.

HOT OLIVE CHEESE PUFFS
Marilyn Davis

Blend:
3 tbsp. soft butter
Add:
1/2 c. sifted flour
1/2 tsp. paprika
1 c. grated cheddar cheese

1/4 tsp. salt

Shape around 2 1/2 dozen olives. Bake at 400° for 10 to 15 minutes.

PEAR RELISH
Mrs. Julian L. Gray

4 quarts sliced pears
3 oranges and 1 lemon, ground in food chopper
1 large can crushed pineapple
1 small bottle cherries
3/4 c. sugar to each cup of mixture

Mix all ingredients together (except cherries) and cook about 2 hours. Put in cherries just before removing from heat. Fills 8 pint jars.

ORANGE JULIUS
Debi Hooper

1/3 (6 oz.) can orange juice
   concentrate
1/2 c. milk
1/2 c. water
1/2 tsp. vanilla
1/4 c. sugar
1 egg

   Put ingredients in blender, blend thoroughly. May add ice cubes also. Double ingredients to make blenderful.
   Serve immediately.

SUNSHINE TEA
Lee Warren

4 Lipton tea bags
1 quart cold water from tap
2 tbsp. sugar (or more)

   Fill quart jar of water, drop in tea bags, add sugar and let stand upside down in sun for 6 or 8 hours. Shake once or twice during day.

DIABETIC AND LOW CALORIE

BEEF-A-LA-JUNE
Gertrude Patenaude

14 oz. cube steak or chuck steak (remove any fat)
1 large pepper
1 large onion
Tomato juice

Dice pepper, onion and steak. Spray pan with Pam. Brown onion, pepper and steak. Pour in enough tomato juice to cover ingredients. Cover and simmer 1 to 1 1/2 hours or till tender. Serves 2.

CABBAGE-BEEF CASSEROLE
Gertrude Patenaude

14 oz. ground chuck
1 medium onion
6 c. shredded cabbage
12 oz. tomato juice
Dash of pepper and oregano

Place in baking dish and cover. Bake at 350° for 1 1/2 hours if you like cabbage, cooked well, or 1 hour for chewy cabbage.

CHEESE AND SAUSAGE CUSTARD
Georgia Simons

1 (8 oz.) pkg. Brown n' Serve sausages
6 eggs
Salt and pepper
1 c. grated cheddar cheese
1/2 c. whipping cream
1 tbsp. minced chives and parsley, mixed

Slice sausages diagonally and brown in frying pan. Beat eggs, cream, salt, pepper and chives and parsley together. Sprinkle 1/2 cheese over sausages. Pour egg mixture on top. Sprinkle with remaining cheese. Cook uncovered over low heat without stirring until set, about 25 minutes. Place under broiler until browned. Serve in wedges. 4 servings. 0 carbohydrates per servings.

BROILED CHICKEN SALAD
Georgia Simons

2 c. diced cooked chicken
1 1/2 c. diced celery
1/2 c. mayonnaise
1/4 c. slivered almonds, toasted
1/4 c. French Dressing
Salt, pepper to taste
1/3 c. sour cream
1 c. grated cheese

(CONT'D)

Broiled Chicken Salad (CONT'D)

French Dressing:
2/3 c. olive or vegetable oil
1/3 c. wine vinegar
Season with salt and pepper and
    marjoram to taste
1 mashed clove garlic
1/4 tsp. paprika

Marinate chicken and celery in French dressing 1 hour. Mix mayonnaise and sour cream. Add to chicken. Mix lightly. Sprinkle with almonds. Chill. Put in 9 inch pie plate. Cover with cheese. Place under broiler until cheese melts. Serve at once. 4 servings. 4 grams carbohydrates per serving.

SHRIMP EGG FOO YONG
Joy Huggett

6 eggs
1 c. shrimp, diced
1 c. bean sprouts, drained
1/2 c. onion, chopped
1/2 tsp. salt
1 tbsp. vegetable oil

Beat eggs. Stir in bean sprouts, shrimp, onion and salt. Cook in heavy skillet in 1 tbsp. oil (add more when needed). Use about 3 tbsp. of mixture per "pancake".

Serve with sauce: blend 2 tsp. cornstarch with 3/4 c. water. Add 1 bouillon cube, 2 tsp. soy sauce, 1 tsp. vinegar and 1 tsp. sugar (or substitute). Cook, stirring constantly until it bubbles 1 minute.

APPLE MUFFINS
Gertrude Patenaude

4 eggs
2 to 3 pkgs. sweetener
4 slices whole wheat bread
4 apples, peeled and cubed
Cinnamon to taste

Combine all ingredients in blender except apples (stir in by hand). Pour into 8 muffin tins. (Use Pam on Teflon tins.) Bake 45 minutes at 350°. 2 muffins equal 1 breakfast of 1 egg, 1 fruit and 1 bread.

APPLE PIE
                                                    Elsie Logston

6 apples, peeled and sliced for pie   4 tbsp. water
2 tbsp. Sweet 10

Roll apples in 1 tsp. cinnamon and 1/4 tsp. allspice. Mix Sweet 10 and water and pour over. Bake in double pie shell at 425° for 35 to 45 minutes.

BANANA CREAM PIE

3 eggs   3/4 tsp. vanilla
Dash salt   1 c. sliced bananas
1/2 c. evaporated skim milk   1 tbsp. lemon juice
1 1/4 c. fresh skim milk   9 inch graham cracker crust
Powdered sweetener equivalent to
    1/2 c. sugar

Beat eggs with salt and evaporated milk until well mixed. Add fresh milk and powdered sweetener. Cook in top of double boiler until mixture is consistency of soft custard. Add vanilla, mix well and remove from heat. Toss sliced bananas with lemon juice and arrange in bottom of graham cracker crust, reserving slices for garnish. Pour custard mix over the bananas. Arrange reserved slices over the top and chill until set.

COCKEYED CAKE
                                                    Louelle Midgett

1 1/2 c. flour   5 tbsp. cooking oil
3 tbsp. cocoa   1 tbsp. vinegar
4 tsp. Sweet'N'Low   1 tsp. vanilla
1 tsp. soda   1 c. cold water

Combine flour, cocoa, soda and Sweet'N'Low in greased square pan. Makes three grooves in dry mixture. Into one pour oil, next vinegar, then the vanilla. Pour cold water over all. Beat until smooth. Bake at 350° for half an hour (30 minutes).

GRAHAM CRACKER CRUST

1 1/2 c. fine graham cracker crumbs   4 tbsp. margarine

    Mix well and press into 9 inch pie plate. Use another plate of equal size to pack crumbs in firmly. Chill or freeze until ready to use. Serves 8.

    One slice (1/8 crust) contains: 22 grams carbohydrates, 7 grams protein, 16 grams fat, and 260 calories.

    Exchange value: 1 slice (1/8 crust) equals 1 bread, 1/2 milk, and 2 fat.

MOUSSE AU CHOCOLAT   Georgia Simons

1 egg white beaten till stiff   1 small container Cool Whip,
2 tsp. cocoa   softened
Dash of nutmeg

    Whip egg white until stiff adding nutmeg and cocoa towards end of whipping. Fold into Cool Whip. Cover and refrigerate until set up. Serves 4.

PEACH PARFAIT   Georgia Simons

2 jars baby peaches, small   1 small container Cool Whip

    Fill 4 parfait or water glasses with alternate peaches and whipped topping. Refrigerate until cool through. Serves 4. Low in carbohydrates.

PINENIBBLES   Gertrude Patenaude

1 average can crushed pineapple   1 tbsp. lemon juice
4 envelopes unflavored gelatin   2 or 3 pkgs. sweetener

    Drain juice into pan. Add gelatin and 1/2 of pineapple. Heat and stir till gelatin dissolves. Add sugar substitute, lemon and rest of pineapple. Place in 8 inch pan and place in refrigerator. Cut into 25 squares. 5 squares equals 1 fruit.

PINEAPPLE CHEESE PIE
Gertrude Patenaude

1 large can sliced pineapple in juice
8 oz. Farmer's cheese
2 pkgs. Sweet N' Low
1 pkg. unflavored gelatin

Drain pineapple juice into small saucepan. Add Sweet N'Low and gelatin and set aside. Cube pineapple. Blend pineapple and cheese in blender until smooth. Bring juice, Sweet N' Low and gelatin to a boil, stirring with a spoon or whisk. Add to cheese mixture in blender and blend until smooth. Pour mixture into sprayed pie plate and chill. Slice into wedges to serve.

In season garnish each wedge with a sliced fresh strawberry. When fresh strawberries are not available, a little diet strawberry jam adds color.

SQUASH PIE
Elsie Logston

3 eggs
1 1/2 c. squash
2 Saccharin pills, 1 1/4 tsp. Sweet 10
1 c. milk
1 tsp. cinnamon
1/4 tsp. nutmeg
1/4 tsp. ginger
1/4 tsp. cloves

Mix well and bake in pie shell at $400°$ till set, about 45 minutes.

PIE CRUST - 9 inch shell
Elsie Logston

1 1/3 c. flour
1/3 c. corn oil
1/2 tsp. salt
3 tbsp. milk

Mix ingredients well and roll out on wax paper.

STRAWBERRY CREAM PIE
Gertrude Patenaude

1 c. fresh strawberries (use sugar twin to sweeten)
2 large containers Cool Whip
1 container low fat strawberry yogurt
1 chocolate pie shell or 1 graham cracker shell

Mix together 1/2 c. fresh strawberries, 1 container Cool Whip and container of low fat strawberry yogurt. Place mixture in pie shell and freeze. When ready to serve, thaw for about 20 to 30

(CONT'D)

Strawberry Cream Pie (CONT'D)

minutes. Then put a scoop of Cool Whip (refrigerated) on top of each serving piece. Then put 1 tablespoon of strawberries on the Cool Whip.

This recipe may be used with any kind of fruit yogurt and any kind of fresh fruit. Delicious!

ZABAGLIONE   Georgia Simons

4 egg yolks (large eggs   2 tsp. vanilla
4 tbsp. honey

Place first 2 ingredients over medium direct heat and bring to gentle boil, beating constantly until thick and fluffy. Add vanilla. Put in sherbert glasses. Serves 4; either hot or cold. Low in carbohydrates.

FRESH STRAWBERRY JAM

2 1/2 c. fresh strawberries   1 tsp. cornstarch
    (or frozen dry pack)   Liquid sweetener equivalent to
2 tbsp. lemon juice   1/3 c. sugar

Combine all ingredients except sweetener in a saucepan and simmer for 20 minutes, stirring frequently. Skim and discard any foam that has accumulated. Remove from heat and cool slightly. Add liquid sweetener 1/2 tsp. at a time, tasting after each addition until desired sweetness is reached. Store in refrigerator. This jam will not freeze successfully. Makes 2 cups.

DARE BUILDING SUPPLY

BUXTON, N. C.
27920

FREE DELIVERY TO OCRACOKE ISLAND

EVERYTHING FOR THE BUILDER

Phone 995-5715

Edward Midgett — Fred Neuman

Directly on the ocean front, we offer a complete vacation complex here on the real outer banks of North Carolina.

Hatteras Island Motel
Restaurant & Fishing Pier

Post Office Box 8
Rodanthe, North Carolina 27968

Telephone: (919) 987-2345 - Motel
(919) 987-2323 - Fishing Pier

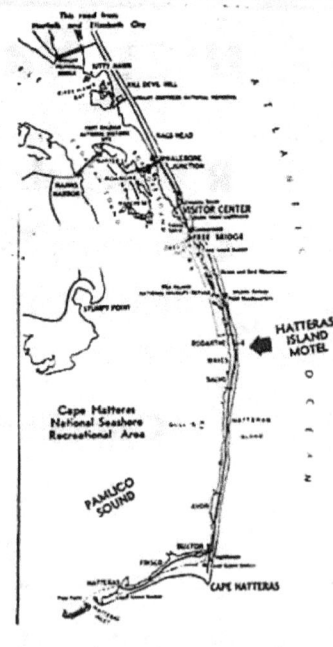

919-441-5792
P.O. Box 623
Nags Head, N.C. 27959

804-481-0270
2117 Kendall Circle East
Virginia Beach, Va. 23451

MEEKINS
Realty Corporation

11 Mile Post 158 By Pass
Nags Head, N.C.

ALTON W. MEEKINS   MARIAN K. MEEKINS

Outer Banks Camper Center

R V Repair Parts   **Tents, Tent Poles**
Coleman Products   **Stakes & Guy Lines**
and Repair Parts   **Pipe and Fittings**

Camping Supplies For All Your Needs

"THE HUGGETTS"
Joy, Bob, Susi, and Robert

Cope Hatteras   Box 87   Rodanthe, N.C. 27968

Outer Banks Camper Service, Inc.
Leisure Homes Sales Service

- Campers
- Mobile Homes
- Double Wides
- Modulars

"Where service after the sale is not forgotten"

Radio Dispatched

(919) 987-2318 (919) 987-2272
Cape Hatteras Box 25
Rodanthe, N.C. 27968

N.C. Lic. No. 01917

SALES & RENTALS
BUILDERS

REAL ESTATE
LOTS & COTTAGES

Midgett Realty
R REALTOR

The Cape Hatteras Lighthouse stands today as both a landmark and part of the history of the Outer Banks. It is a fitting symbol for Midgett Realty.

We know the Outer Banks so, because our family has lived here so long. The Midgett name is part of Outer Banks History, and we have a proud heritage to live up to. With 4 offices to serve you, we are constantly striving to live up to that name.

If you're looking for real estate, a home or just a cottage to rent, come talk to Midgett Realty — we know the Outer Banks....
...and we know real estate.

Main Office
986-2141
P.O. Box 128
Hatteras, N.C. 27943

995-5333
P.O. Box 60
Avon, N.C. 27915

Area Code
(919)

441-6666
P.O. Box 1066
Kill Devil Hills, N.C. 27948

987-2350
P.O. Box 61
Rodanthe, N.C. 27968

Murray Auto Supply inc.

Manteo: 473-3466
473-5861
Kill Devil Hills: 441-7163
Hatteras: 995-4121

PLANTERS NATIONAL BANK

Member FDIC

MANTEO
473-2181

NAGS HEAD
441-5561

BUXTON
995-5811

KITTY HAWK
(coming soon)

MASTERCARD   VISA

the BLUE WHALE
SALVO, NORTH CAROLINA

Covey's Repair & Construction

Specializing in
House Piling, Banding,
Bulkheading

Pete, Owner
Box 74
Rodanthe, N.C. 27968
(919) 987-2370

The OCEAN AIRE MOTEL

Air Conditioned - TV - Central Heat
Picnic and Swimming area
Children's Play Ground

Boats For Rent

— Open All Year —
Phone: 987-2244

Rodanthe, N.C.
Lovie and Valton Midgett, Mgr.

Cape Hatteras KOA
P.O. Box 43
Rodanthe, N.C. 27968

Phone: KOA-Holiday (919) 987-2307
KOA-Original (919) 987-2250

John & Joan Berry, Managers

Capt. John Allen Motel

Room & Efficiences
SEA CHEST GIFT SHOP
Antique - Souvenir
Beach & Fishing Supply
CAPE HATTERAS ISLAND
Box 98 - Hwy. 12
Rodanthe, NC 27968
Myrna & Tom Peters   919-987-2303

Mollie A. Fearing and Associates, Inc.

THE INSURANCE HOUSE
owned by:
Mollie A. Fearing—Broker
Beth B. Elliot—Agent
Grizelle B. Fearing—Agent
Linda Pledger—Bookkeeper

Box 1188
411 Agona St.
Manteo, N.C.

Bus. 473-3476
Res. 473-2908

KELLOGG
SUPPLY COMPANY, INC.

Our 35th Anniversary
1946 - 1981

**LUMBER ● HARDWARE
POWER TOOLS ● FIXTURES**

From Materials to Homes
BUILDING IS PROGRESS

FOR THE INDIVIDUAL
   FOR THE COUNTRY
      FOR THE AREA

MANTEO, N.C. PHONE 473-2167	**FREE DELIVERY**	2 Locations to Serve You Kill Devil Hills, N.C. Phone 441-4324

"EVERYTHING TO BUILD ANYTHING"

QUARTERDECK RESTAURANT

*Finest Hatteras Seafood
Char-broiled Steaks
Italian Specials Daily
Full-Service Restaurant
Dinner Music*

FRISCO, NORTH CAROLINA
Hwy. 12, ½ mile south Frisco Post Office
986-2425

Your Hosts:
Russ & Gina Ochs

Ice, Groceries, Bait
Tackle, Guns & Aummunition

Frisco Shopping Center

P.O. Box 10
Frisco, N.C. 27936
Telephone: (919) 995-5022

Beach Vehicle Rentals

JOBOB'S
Trading Post

Fresh Seafood
Tackle-Hardware-Groceries
Bait-Ice

Rodanthe, N.C.
987-2201

Outer Beaches Realty, Inc.

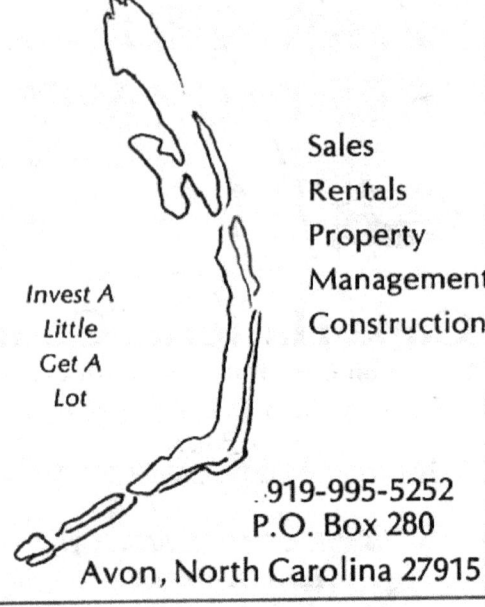

Sales
Rentals
Property
Management
Construction

Invest A Little Get A Lot

919-995-5252
P.O. Box 280
Avon, North Carolina 27915

FROGGY DOG
Restaurant

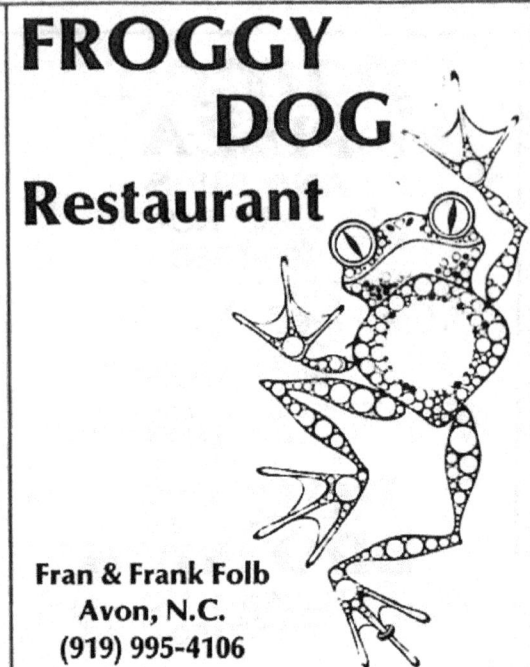

Fran & Frank Folb
Avon, N.C.
(919) 995-4106

AUSTIN REALTY CO.

Edith Karen Austin
Broker

Sales, Rentals
Year-round Maintenance
& Security

Phone: 919-987-2208
Salvo, N.C.

THE BOARDWALK
Family Restaurant

**Kinnakeet Shopping Village
AVON**

Breakfast 6 a.m.   Lunch 11 a.m. - 3 p.m.
Dinner 5 p.m. - 9 p.m.

— Home Cooking —

ROCCO'S PIZZA
AND SUBS
Avon, NC
995-5358

FRESH DOUGH

ROCCO'S BROTHER
Hatteras, NC
986-2150

— For The Very Best Italian Food —

Tennis
Swimming Pool
Right on Ocean

Cape Hatteras Court
Buxton on Cape Hatteras, North Carolina

P.O. Box 339
BUXTON, NORTH CAROLINA 27920

DAVE & CAROL DAWSON
Phone (919) 995-5611

WELCOME TO CAPE HATTERAS
AVON SHOPPING CENTER
Avon, N.C.

BAIT & TACKLE
SUPERMARKET
SENTRY HARDWARE
— FRESH MEAT —

Telephone 995-5362
Mike & Charles Williams, Manager

The VILLAGE SHOP

The Village Shop
AVON, NC
Located In
Kinnakeet Shopping Village
N.C. 12

Nautical and Unusual Gifts
Leather — Clothing
Crafts — Shells

Browers Welcome   Phone 995-5252

RED DRUM EXXON

Ch 13 KQK 3842
Mechanic on Duty
Beach Towing Service
Automotive Service
and Repair
995-5646

Kentucky Fried Chicken

"It's finger-lickin' good"

BUXTON, on Cape Hatteras
Phone 995-5281

Juanita Peele
and
Meline Whittle

Conners Cape Hatteras Supermarket

Buxton, N.C.
Tel: 995-5711

WILLIS BOAT LANDING

Johnson Motors
Galvanized Trailers
Sea-Ox Boats - Dixie Boats
Volvo Sales & Service

Marine and Hunting Supplies
Boat Rentals   Motor Repairs

OPEN YEAR 'ROUND
Phone 986-2208   Hatteras, NC

Phone: 919-986-2532
Complete Marina Facilities
P.O. Box 87
Hatteras, N.C. 27943

HATTERAS FISHING CENTER, Inc.

Boat Slips
Camper Park
Charter Boats
Shower House

Tackle Shop
Ramp Service
Self Service Fuel
Ice & Bait

Dry Storage for Boats & Campers
Hunting & Fishing Information

HATTERAS, N.C.

TACKLE SHOP
Best Tackle Shop On The Coast

Antiques, Nauticals, Decoys

Paintings, Carvings
Island Crafts

The Barking Fish

Eleanor L. Cushing, *Proprietor*
41 mi south of Oregon Inlet
at
Buxton-on-Hatteras Island

P.O. Box 354
Buxton-on-Hatteras Island
North Carolina 27920

Telephone
919-995-5927

OPEN YEAR AROUND

Stratford at Avon Theatre

Box 220
Avon, N.C. 27915
Phone: 919-995-5323

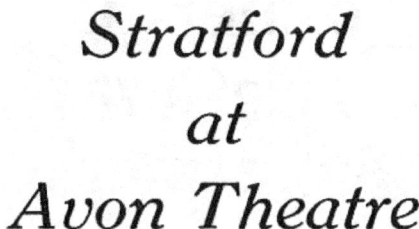

Compliments of

Tower Circle Motel

P.O. Box 88 - Buxton, N.C. 27920

Jack and Mary Gray
Managers

Phone: 995-5353
Area Code 919

Gifts — Housewares
Gourmet Gifts
Interior Design
Paints — Hardware
Fashions — Cosmetics
Pharmacy

"Your everything store"

Fearing's, Inc.
manteo, north carolina 27954

(919) 473-2149

OUTER BANKS INSURANCE agency incorporated

Keeping watch over you and yours-

101 BUDLEIGH ST.
P.O. BOX 759
MANTEO, N.C. 27954
(919) 473-3463

M. KEITH FEARING, JR.
PRES.
LARRY D. WHITT
MGR.

JACOCKS PHARMACY NO. 2
Mile Post 1 - Kitty Hawk, N.C.
Phone: 261-3333

MILLERS PHARMACY
on the beach m.p. 11
Nags Head, N.C.
Phone: 441-7228

**Dare Air Heating
and
Air Conditioning**

P.O. Box 201, Hatteras, N.C.

Serving The People Of Hatteras Island
For Over Fifteen Years

For Sales & Service - Call 986-2420

N.C. Lic. No. 4805 - Active 1971

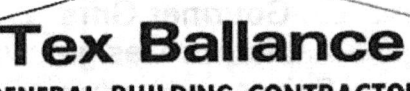

Tex Ballance
GENERAL BUILDING CONTRACTOR

Box 175
HATTERAS, N. C.
Ph. 919/986-2319

Lamps * Seashells * Driftwood * Shell Jewelry
All Year Mail Order Service
Gifts Of All Kinds - Live Hermit Crabs

W.S. Stetson
Tel. 473-2976
441-5739

"STETSON'S"
THE SHIPWRECK
On Nags Head-Manteo Causeway
Nags Head, N.C. 27959

MAIN HIGHWAY 64
P.O. Box 515
Manteo, N.C.

FOOD-A-RAMA
IGA. INC.

U.S. 64 EAST
MANTEO, NC 27954
(919) 473-3219

A & B Carpets, Inc.
SPECIALIZING IN ALL TYPES OF FLOORCOVERING
SALES - INSTALLATION - CARPET CLEANING
CARPET BINDING & WALLPAPER

FRANKLIN ADAMS
RES. 473-5550

TOMMY BARNES
RES. 473-3308

E. Crouse Gray, Jr.

NAGS HEAD PROFESSIONAL BUILDING
NAGS HEAD, N.C. 27959

ATTORNEY AT LAW

Post Office Box 177
Telephone (919) 441-4338

Herbert L. Thomas   Attorney-At-Law

Evans Building
Manteo, N.C. 27954
919-473-3426

Medical Center
Hatteras, N.C.
919-986-2443

Cape Sandbox Motel

Toni Zindell, Owner

Buxton, N.C. 27920
919-995-5785

Gae Zindell, Manager

BOX 412 HATTERAS, N.C. 27943
Phone: (919) 986-2505
Ellis Flinchum, Mgr.

surf-n-sound camping

G. IRVIN ALDRIDGE
ATTORNEY AND COUNSELLOR AT LAW
ALDRIDGE, SEAWELL, & KHOURY

VIRGINIA DARE ROAD
P.O. BOX 339
MANTEO, N.C. 27954

Office: 919-473-3484
473-3445
Residence: 473-2207

Hatteras Island — Full Hookups

FRISCO WOODS CAMPGROUNDS, INC.
"WE'VE PUT THE CAMP BACK IN CAMPING"
"TENTERS WE LOVE YOU"

Box 159
Frisco, N.C. 27936

Ward & Betty Barnett
(919) 995-5208

MANTEO FURNITURE COMPANY, INC.
Home of Fine Furniture & Appliances
Name Brands of Floor Coverings - Vinyls and Carpeting
Sales & Installation   Toll Free No: 995-5689

HATTERAS WASH BASKET INC.
COIN OPERATED LAUNDERMAT ● SELF SERVICE ● OPEN ALL YEAR
MOTEL LINEN SERVICE ● SERVING HATTERAS ISLAND
GARLAND and KAREN MIDGETTE

BUXTON, N.C.

THE WHATZIT SHOP
—Featuring—
NEEDLE ARTS

canvas & crewel embroidery, yarns 'n stuff, classes & private instructions in Buxton - on the back road

---

Phone: 986-2363-Home 986-2248 T.V.-Wall to Wall Carpets, Air Conditioned, Steam Heat, Tiled Baths

BURRUS MOTOR COURT

David Burrus
1 mi from Ocracoke Ferry

"Overlooking Pamlico Sound"
33 Modern Rooms and Apts.   Near Gulf Stream & Inlet Fishing, Swimming Pool

Hatteras, N.C.

SONNY'S WATERFRONT RESTAURANT
Full Line Restaurant
Open from 6 a.m. to 9 p.m.

Tel: (919) 986-2471   Your Host: SONNY QUIDLEY

Compliments of

H. CURTIS GRAY & ASSOCIATES
REAL ESTATE BROKERS
P.O. Box 133
Buxton, N.C. 27920   Phone (919) 995-5779

Ormond's
of Cape Hatteras, Inc.
FASHIONS & GIFTS
P.O. Box 634   Buxton, N.C. 27920

BURRUS

Hatteras, N.C.
Telephone: 986-2333

"Heart of Fishing Country"   Authorized Daiwa Service Center

HATTERAS TACKLE SHOP
P.O. Box 188   Hatteras, N.C. 27943
Custom Made Rods, Reels, Tackle, Bait, Marine Supplies
J.N. "Jap" Needham, Phone (919) 986-2520, C.F. "Fred" Kirkland

LIGHTHOUSE VIEW MOTEL
Modern, Comfortable   Cottages & Rooms   Air Conditioned   By Day or Week
Buxton-on-Cape Hatteras, North Carolina   Phone: (919) 995-5680 -
"BEST WISHES TO RODANTHE & WAVES FIRE DEPARTMENT"

BEACH COMBER

TEXACO

24 hr. Road Service and Beach Towing   Dealer for the Albemarle Boats
Hatteras, N.C. 27943   Night: 995-5540   Day (919) 986-2107

The SEA GULL Motel
Phone: 919-986-2550
Hatteras, N.C. 27943

SEA BIRDS CARDS 'n' GIFTS
Open Year Around
Sea Gate North   5½ Mile Post - Bypass 158   Phone: (919) 441-5223
P.O. Box 289   Kill Devil Hills, N.C. 27948

BEN'S CONSTRUCTION
Ben Marriner
P.O. Box 1109   Hatteras, N.C. 27943   Phone: 986-2267
NEW CONSTRUCTION ● ADDITIONS ● REPAIRS

C.P. Lewis - SURVEYOR
Land Surveying and Planning   Blueprint Service (919) 473-5690
P.O. Box 1030   Budleigh St., Manteo, N.C. 27954
Curtis P. (Scooter) Lewis   NC Reg. Land Surveyor - L-2441

THE CRAFT STUDIO
"a measure of pleasure in creative crafts"
macrame, needleworks, eggeury, yarns, miniatures, trims 'n things, supplies & kits
P.O. Box 64, RODANTHE, N.C. 27968, Phone 919-987-2326   Nancy Howard

JOE'S TEXACO
Major & Minor Repairs - 24 Hour Wrecker Service
Telephone: 987-2239 - Home Telephone: 987-2216

HOOPER GENERAL CONTRACTING
Salvo, North Carolina 27972, (919) 987-2248
*Floor Covering   *Ceramic Tile   *Remodeling

RESIDENTIAL	--Free Estimates--	COMMERCIAL
	RAY BLACK	
	ELECTRICAL CONTRACTOR	
Frisco, N.C. P.O. Box 223,	Serving Hatteras Island	
Phone (919) 995-5408	"You Call Us - We Wire You"	N.C. State Licensed

MOORE'S SHELL
P.O. Box 502, Manteo, N.C. 27954   (919) 441-7502
OPEN ALL YEAR

Rodanthe - Waves	**BILL SAWYER'S PLACE**	Hatteras Island
	Box 86, Rodanthe, N.C. 27968, (919) 987-2214	
TACKLE SHOP - Everything for the Fisherman		SUB-PIZZA SHOP - The Best on the Outer Banks

NEW HORIZONS

Bob Huggett P.O. Box 87 Rodanthe, N.C. 27968 (919) 987-2417
Outer Banks   Rod Holders   WD-40

Waterfall Slide

at Rodanthe on Hatteras Island
(Mention cookbook and receive 50¢ discount)

BURTON K. MYERS, C.P.A.
5908 Columbia Pike
Falls Church, Virginia 22041

Burton Myers Company
Certified Public Accountants

CPA North Carolina and Virginia   931-3000   Home: 703-256-8652

OUTER BANKS MOTEL
Buxton, Cape Hatteras, N.C. 27920

Write or Phone Area Code 919-995-5601
Mrs. Bill Dillon, P.O. Box 428, Buxton, N.C. 27920

Rooms-Efficiencies
2 & 3 Bedroom Cottages

BEN   FRANKLIN

MANTEO
on
Roanoke Island

A
N
D

NAGS HEAD
Milepost 10
On The By-Pass

On Ocean Side

J. & A. EFFICIENCIES
Mr. & Mrs. Earl O'Neal, Owners

Salvo, N.C. 987-2367

Seid Wood Products
P.O. Box 235
Claremont, Va. 23899

804-866-8905
Bobby P. Seid
Evelyn Seid

Groceries & Tackle & Gas
Hatteras, N.C.

for fishin' info:
986-2213

Pelican's Roost

BAKERY

ORANGE BLOSSOM PASTRY SHOP
BIRTHDAY CAKES • PASTRY • WEDDING CAKES

CATERING
HUNDLEY & OAKHAM
BUXTON, N.C.
995-4109

B & M BEACH MART

Home of Conner Lures — Groceries - Notions

Telephone: 995-5589

Bait - Tackle - Ice — Open 7 - 11

PIRATE'S CHEST GIFT SHOP
Welcomes Anglers

Paintings & Prints By Local Artists
Crafts—Art Supplies And Shells
Antiques & T-Shirts

Owners
ODESSA and JOHN WASILI
Phone: 995-5118

FRISCO, N.C. 27936

CRICKET'S SUB SHOP
Subs and Pizza
Buxton, N.C. (919) 995-9463

MOODS INTERIORS & ARTS

Jeannine Metivier
DESIGNER
Ph: 919-995-4170

CURTAINS • WALLPAPER • ART • GIFTS
Open All Year

P.O. Box 636
Buxton, N.C.
27910

SALVO MARKET & MARINA

Fishing Tackle, Beach Supplies
Groceries, Travel Trailer Facilities, Boat Ramp, Docks

EXXON

Salvo, North Carolina 27972

(919) 987-2327

SURF OR SOUND, LTD.
P.O. Box 100, Avon, N. Carolina 27915
Office: 919 995-5801 — Residence: 919/995-5975

HATTERAS ISLAND PROPERTY MANAGEMENT
Sales · Rentals · Insurance
John & Brenda Sitz

POLYNESIAN VILLAS
Avon, N.C.

Cottage Rentals
Day or Week

Open Year Around
919-995-4275

ODEN FISH & OIL CO., INC.
Box 278
HATTERAS, N. C. 27943
Phone 986-2555

Petroleum Products for
Home — Marine — Industry

RED DRUM FOOD MART

Buxton, N.C.   Phone: 995-5721

Full line of groceries, drugs, hardware, fresh produce, cold drinks, beer, wine, kiddy's toys, magazines, choice meats cut to order.

Beach supplies, Open 7 - 11   7 days a week

George O'Neal, owner

- Available to individuals separately or jointly and to nonprofit organizations.
- No service charge if $300 minimum balance is maintained. If balance falls below required minimum anytime during the month your account is charged $5.
- No per item check charge.
- 6% interest compounded continuously, paid on your checking account funds.
- Funds insured to $100,000 by the N.C. Savings Guaranty Corporation.
- Over 59? No minimum balance required and no service fee charged.
- Open Monday through Friday from 1-3 for added convenience.

THE AFFORDABLE CHECKING ACCOUNT

F.O. Box 1050 Highway 64, Manteo, N.C.

Hours:
Mon - Thurs. 9-5
Fri. 9-6

Phone 919 473-5871

- Direct Deposit of Social Security, Civil Service, and other benefit payments into your account.
- Monthly statement mailed to you with complete list of deposits made, checks paid, and interest earned. Paid checks are returned with your statement.
- Personalized checks at low cost. Earnings from your 6-month Money Market Certificates can be transferred automatically to your checking account.
- A money market rate is paid when you open our PERFORMANCE CHECKING account and maintain a $3,500.00 minimum balance.
- No other bank or savings and loan in Eastern North Carolina offers checking with as high a rate of interest and as low a minimum balance as does Eastern Savings.

Sales, Rentals and Cottage Construction

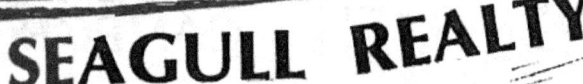

SEAGULL REALTY

Box 3566
Waves, N.C. 27982
Ph. 919-987-2258

Hatteras Island
(located inside Oceanside Art Gallery)

Ruth Ann Burgess
Realtor

Shore Trucking, Inc.

Topsoil, Rock & Gravel
Driveways

Clear Land
Landscaping

Hatteras Island
Seagull Realty
Waves, N.C. 27982
(919) 987-2258

Edenton
Box 271
Edenton, N.C.
(919) 221-4290

"A Good Fishing Spot" On Ocean Side
Mr. & Mrs. E. Burgess Hooper, Owners
Ph: (919) 987-2240 · Salvo, N.C.

SALVO INN MOTEL

E. P. (Paul) Breaux, Jr., President
BOX S, KILL DEVIL HILLS, NC 27948
OFFICE (919) 441-7031 • HOME (919) 441-6535

at Waves on Hatteras Island

Family Style Buffets. Help yourself and run have fun or visit awhile and share a smile. Family Reunion every day, Breakfast like Grandma's; homemade jams, jellies, and preserves. Lunch Like Dinner on the Ground, Emily's Fried Chicken. Quiet Evening Meals. Hatteras Seafoods and Plain Folks Food. Home Cooking by the Sea. Busses and large groups welcome. You won't believe the prices! Emily Landrum (919) 987-2383.

Closed Mondays
Breakfast 7:00-11:00 Lunch 11:30-2:00 Dinner 5:00-9:00

NORTH BEACH CAMPGROUND

GENERAL STORE
Hatteras Island
Rodanthe, N.C.

Bait · Tackle · Ice
Souvenirs · Groceries
Camping Supplies
Hardware · Gifts

HATTERAS ISLAND EMERGENCY NUMBERS

FIRE DEPARTMENT
Rodanthe & Waves .... (987)-2444, 2417, 2370, 2493
Salvo .... (987)-2208, 2248, 2283
Avon 986-2144
Buxton 995-5960
Frisco 995-5121
Hatteras 986-2500
Doctor 986-2388
Sheriffs' Department .... 986-2144 (Ambulance & Rescue)
Coast Guard 987-2311
Park Service Ranger .... 995-5044; night, 995-5033
Veterinarian 986-2452

About the Author

Tom Kelchner, a native of Pennsylvania, writes about the food and drink of everyday life and their historical background. He blogs at PaFoodLife.com and is the author of *Chicamacomico Cookery* (Vol. One) and *To Great Grandmother's House We Go,* a cookbook and food history book based on the vast archive of 1,400 recipes left by his mother-in-law.

He is a retired journalist, blogger and research analyst. He also is an avid, life-long cook and baker, specializing in dishes of the many ethnic groups who settled in Pennsylvania, including the Pennsylvania Dutch.

He first fell in love with the North Carolina Outer Banks in 1964 on a whimsical Saturday jaunt with several fellow sailors when he was stationed at the U.S. Navy Base at Dam Neck.

He described it:

"It was in October and it rained most of the time we were there. We slept in a station wagon in the parking lot of a grocery market, possibly the one on the Beach Road at Jennette's Pier. On the drive down to the Hatteras light house, I remember the amazing beauty and solitude, mile after mile.

"My wife, our dogs and I have been taking off-season vacations to Nags Head for 30 years now. We go in May and October and always stay in efficiencies or rental houses, so I can cook all that fabulous fresh fish."

"The Outer Banks are an amazing place and I hope these facsimile editions help preserve part of its history."

www.ingramcontent.com/pod-product-compliance
Lightning Source LLC
Chambersburg PA
CBHW071857070526
44583CB00016B/1727